W9-DIM-752

JUAN DE MAIRENA

ANTONIO MACHADO

ANTONIO MACHADO

EPIGRAMS, MAXIMS, MEMORANDA, AND MEMOIRS
OF AN APOCRYPHAL PROFESSOR
WITH
AN APPENDIX OF POEMS FROM
The Apocryphal Songbooks

EDITED AND TRANSLATED BY
BEN BELITT

UNIVERSITY OF CALIFORNIA PRESS
BERKELEY AND LOS ANGELES 1963

UNIVERSITY OF CALIFORNIA PRESS
BERKELEY AND LOS ANGELES, CALIFORNIA

CAMBRIDGE UNIVERSITY PRESS
LONDON, ENGLAND

LIBRARY OF CONGRESS CATALOG CARD NUMBER 63-19879
DESIGNED BY ADRIAN WILSON
PRINTED IN THE UNITED STATES OF AMERICA

For William Troy

To whom poets and poetry are indebted

Foreword

Antonio Machado is not only a major lyric poet of Spanish literature but, in the degree to which poetry may be said to engage the metaphysical intuition itself, its exemplary poet-philosopher. At once traditional and modern, meditative and moody, alert to untried modes of expression without forfeiting any of the graces prized by his predecessors, his poetic utterance is linked to the great lyricists of the *siglos de oro.* His obscure provincial life, his expressive subtlety of form, together with the absence of those windfalls which give passing luster to lesser reputations—international prizes, translations, and the like, all of which he seems to have regarded with indifference—these have not served to launch him far beyond the closed circle of Hispanic letters in spite of his manifest greatness. The present translation of his prose work—surely as important as his poetry, if not at times more so, as I shall presently try to make clear—renders Machado something of the belated justice due him.

In a life span extending from 1875 to 1939, the thrust of his talent begins at a point in Spanish history which can hardly be called propitious: the low tide of Spanish intellect which touched bottom in 1898, the year of the Spanish-American War and the surrender of Spain's remaining colonial possessions. His genius reaches its peak in the tense years of the Republic, when matters had taken a brisker turn for his countrymen and contemporaries; and his life was swept away in the tempest of civil war. The drama of Antonio Machado, then, apart from the stresses of his personal struggle—which have their own kind of drama, for all their lack of anecdotal detail—is the drama of Spain itself. His was a sensibility sad by nature and saddened by contingency. His poetry is characterized by a stoicism of surpassing humanity and sublimity: an Attic stoicism, if we may call it that, in the style of Epictetus rather than in the Roman manner of Seneca. It is a classical stoicism crossed by distinctively Spanish modes of feeling and reasoning, like the comedy of Cervantes' *Quijote* and his lesser novels, combining man's cunning and man's spiritual nobility in the presence of human suffering, with an insight into human frailties that begins in the act of understanding one's own. This implies ethical commitment; and it is precisely on such a groundwork that the poet Machado initiates his search for ontological answers to the questions of why men are as they are and not otherwise. In *Juan de Mairena* we have, set forth in the highly personalized inflection of his prose, certain of his answers.

The fact that Antonio Machado was educated in Madrid at the Institución Libre de Enseñanza, whose heterodox stand in relation to prevailing educational norms is well known, is in itself significant in the development of a potential scholar. There he learned, above all things, that education is not the quantitative sum of accumulated knowledge, but a totality, a *paideia* that enriches man as an individual and as a social entity. Appointed in 1907 to the post of teacher of French in the public school of Soria—that "high and cold" province of Castile—and removed from the turmoil of metropolitan life, he devoted himself to teaching and to weaving his poetical web. There he married a young girl of Soria with whom he was deeply in love, and there too he lost her after a harrowing illness, turning himself forever after into that inconsolable widower visible underneath the whole fabric of his poetry: a widower meditating the meaning of love, the beloved, and the transcendence of eros as one of the expressive forms of being.

In 1910 he studied philosophy in Paris under Bédier and Bergson. On his return to Spain, however, never having received his doctorate, he was disqualified from teaching in the area for which he felt a special vocation. Doubtless this frustration enriched his poetical and critical accomplishment in the years to come. Assigned to teach French in the Andalusian city of Baeza, he alternated the chore of language teaching with the teaching of Spanish literature. He was ultimately transferred to posts in Segovia and Madrid. Such, in brief, was the pattern of

Machado's life: muted, gray, taciturn, lived, as it were, against the grain of the large city, the amenities of occasional fame, and the literary coteries. In a word, Machado was the epitome of the provincial schoolteacher—

> a teacher
> of living languages (yesterday's
> master of minstrelsy,
> the nightingale's apprentice)
> in a village chilly and dank,
> lugubrious, bereft

—notwithstanding the fact that in 1934 he was elected to the Spanish Academy and enjoyed a well-earned prestige among a cultivated Spanish minority. Later, caught up in the whirlwind of civil war, he became a voluntary expatriate to France, where in 1939 he died in the little village of Collioure.

The canon of Antonio Machado is a slender one, concentrated into a few books of austere and uneasy poetic texture. Today they compose a single volume often reprinted under the title of *Complete Poems*, into which have been collected his *Soledades* (1903), *Galerías* (1907), *Campos de Castilla* (1912), *Canciones* (1922), and *Nuevas canciones* (1924), together with a handful of fugitive poems from his later years. He also published a series of prose pieces under the title of *Cancionero apócrifo de Abel Martín* (1931) and *Juan de Mairena. Sentencias, donaires, apuntes y recuerdos de un profesor apócrifo* (1936). After his death, further appendixes to *Juan de Mairena* along with some unpublished fragments under the title of *Los complementarios* (1949) were compiled. Mr. Belitt's translation gathers the core of this prose work, nimble, ironical, and unsurpassed in its revelation of the man Machado and his intellectual preoccupations: a profile of his poetical harvest and of twentieth-century Spain. It belongs with the finest Spanish prose works of this century.

One phase of Antonio Machado's work is especially linked to the ideology of his generation. I refer to that select company, later known as the "generation of '98," which made its appearance in the active life of Spain at the close of the nineteenth century—a cadre of talents which took as their special province the whole being of Spain and sought to probe into its history for a deeper understanding of the factors contributing to its decadence after the seventeenth century. It was the hope of this group to fuse the culture of modern Europe with the literary sources and traditional thought of their Spanish heritage and thereby to give new direction to their collective identity. The urgency of their preoccupation can be felt throughout the whole of Machado's poetry—above all, in his *Campos de Castilla:* the landscapes of Castile, the peasants of the moors and the uplands, and the choice of literary themes, medieval, popular, and traditional. More significant still is the reformist bias of the group as a whole which permeates the work of Machado: the notion of a Spain renewed by the self-knowledge of its peoples and its contacts with all that was best in the accomplishment of Europe, its literary, philosophical, and political trends. Whether the generation of '98 diagnosed their ills correctly, or whether their postulates produced any positive results, are questions that need not concern us here. Their imaginative excesses together with a certain lack of expediency, may well have limited the effectiveness of a group inclined to dream and confound their literary vision with the more monotonous chore of remaking a lackadaisical nation. But their ardent good will remains exemplary.

In any event, the Machado preoccupied with sociological and historical considerations, and tapping them for poetic sustenance, is not the primary Machado. His most important and accomplished poems are the lyrics which reveal a contemporanized *homo universalis* expressing himself through the mode of his own humanity. These include the *Soledades, Galerías, Canciones,* and *Nuevas canciones,* together with the magnificent, if at times hermetic, pieces infiltrated into the prose of *Juan de Mairena* and *Abel Martín.* Here is a Machado who commands a profound philosophical vein, speaking in measured and mournful accents that instruct and delight, charging the reader with like melancholy and resignation at the same time that they induce a virile acceptance of life for whatever it may hold of Promethean destiny in the end.

The present translation concerns the reflective and philosophic Machado, and presents one of the most singular inventions in the whole of twentieth-century Spanish literature, *Juan de Mairena.* The imaginary personage who gives his name to this work is a wholly remarkable creation. Springing from the imagination of the author, he takes on an identity that displaces and complements his creator's—becomes, indeed, one of Machado's Others. A study of Machado's "complementaries,"* the fictive identities by whose means the poet sought to resolve what Ortega y Gasset would have called the "perspectivism" of his life, or, as we put matters philosophically today, his Otherness if not in fact his Othernesses—is both intricate and taxing, and might well require a genre of depth psychology to be fully understood. Essentially, it involves a train of deliberate projections, or doubles, of the poet's identity, with the aim of transposing a complex personal dilemma upon a series of imaginary lives. The examples of this tactic outside the sanctum of present-day psychology, are few, nor is the phenomenon usual among men of letters, for whom the pseudonym, as a rule, merely displaces the given name. However, a distinction must be drawn between a pseudonym and a Machadian "complementary." The "complementary," properly speaking, does not provide a substitute for the personality of its creator; rather, its effect is to enrich with new perspectives and afford its "real" counterpart an autonomy of expression that the pseudonym annuls. It is in no sense a pathological double like Dostoevski's Goliadkin or the projections of the schizophrenic, but an objective creation of the conscious will tempered and scaled to paradigms of behavior immanent in the author.

---

*To the most celebrated of Antonio Machado's doubles, Juan de Mairena and Abel Martín, may be added a series which, between the stillborn and those still to be born, runs to a baker's dozen. Guillermo de Torre, in an interesting article entitled "Identity and Doubles in A. Machado," examines the question and catalogues the doubles by name. A. Sánchez Barbudo, in his *Studies of Unamuno and Machado* (Ediciones Guadarrama, Madrid, 1959), also analyzes the theme of the Other in the poet. Both present invaluable data which should be known by all those interested in the problem. (S. S. P.)

Among the doubles of Machado, Juan de Mairena is the most important and representative—so much so, indeed, that without an adequate understanding of this identity, the poetry of Machado would lose much of its resonance and depth. It is Mairena's function, along with Abel Martín, his teacher and fellow contrary, to act as theoretical exegete to the lyrical Machado, unfolding those preoccupations with the Spanish temper so essential to a search for basic social criteria. Personages like Mairena and Martín achieve a singular kind of relief: they are in effect a repertory of living and problematical beings who act as interlocutors of emotive and intellectual predicaments that the poet, for complex and occult reasons of his own, has decided not to engage at first hand. What the intimate being of Machado might have been is difficult to determine in fact, in spite of our proximity to him in time. One might go on to point out that the absence of facile confidences on the part of our writers, and the avoidance of those intimate "keys" so common in other literatures—French, for example—mutually gratifying reader and writer, is the rule rather than the exception in Spanish literature. The Spanish man of letters, whether novelist or poet, is chary of personal reference; he is not partial to the epistolary genre or the memoir; he does not readily confide in his neighbor or colleague. For this reason, the cache of posthumous documents to suggest what manner of man he was while alive is generally scant. We might well intuit that the apocryphal Mairena and Martín function in this instance as screens or masks, at once concealing and provocative, for the personality of their creator. They furnish clues to his temperament and character, given Machado's characteristic introversion and mournful timidity; and they assist in the dialectical unfolding of a mind riddled by insecurity—by ontological and methodological doubts regarding the validity of doubt.

As so often happens with imaginary creations drawn from the deepest fiber of their shaping personality, the figment little by little displaces its creator, until the moment arrives when even his most significant actions and crucial commitments take on the character of an alter ego, giving him a cachet at once dissembling and whimsical while it affords him maximum freedom of expression. There are clearly notions which Machado would never have committed to paper. The recovery of a part of Machado's notebooks and diaries, collected under the title of *Los complementarios* (*The Complementaries*) and dating as far back as 1912, allows us a direct glimpse into this mirror play. It was apparently Machado's way to turn into "apocrypha" aspects of his thinking which, in *Los complementarios,* amount to rough preliminary drafts. There is reason to assume that Juan de Mairena, the poet's most significant "complementary," is a kind of heir of that Machado buried under intimate journals—an heir gifted with a certain audacity, who, armed with the thinking of his benefactor, adds marginal glosses of his own and a bounty of further considerations.

The first problem confronting the biographer of Juan de Mairena might well be to determine what elements of the real Machado are incorporated into the *persona* of his "complementary," in what human model his being is embedded, or if he is indeed only a phantasm with no direct or indirect relation to actuality.

In all probability Juan de Mairena is hewn from the pedagogical block of that very Institución Libre de Enseñanza which showered Machado with so many fruitful illuminations; he is perhaps an amalgam of human types and character traits of his teachers and associates. Teachers like Castillejo, Cossío, Dr. Simarro, Zulueta, and Jiménez may all have left their mark on the apocryphal Mairena. Another seminal figure present in that earlier fiction is Abel Martín, the apocryphal teacher of Mairena, concerning whom we cannot enter into details at the present time. It must suffice to say that Abel Martín, in his earlier epoch, reflects philosophical preoccupations present in the mind of the poet Machado, and functions as his ontological mentor, expounding his thought much as Machado himself might have done it—had he but dared—ex cathedra. Abel Martín—atheist, bachelor, tippler, and connoisseur of Leibnitz —is a forerunner of Mairena for the years just before 1930. Later, when Machado had resolved to participate more openly in the social and human issues which led to the fall of the Spanish monarchy and the inception of a revolutionary phase of republican politics, Juan de Mairena increasingly supersedes Abel Martín, with a corresponding decline of allusions to his apocryphal teacher. In the dramatic interval of the civil war (1936–1939) it is Mairena who obtrudes himself, discusses, conjectures, and declaims, absorbing Machado into himself almost totally; the poet appears in his own guise only as expositor of a handful of his poems, and those by no means his best.

Polemicist, eccentric, and moralist of a sophistical cut that calls to mind certain latecomers to the school that shared Socrates' task of rousing the Athenian spirit, Juan de Mairena is equally partial to scholastic syllogistic discourse and rhetorical gambits in the service of ideas he could not pursue in his poems without the risk of vitiating their force and turning his art into social pedagogy. Through his aid Machado, who had always yearned to profess philosophy professionally, expounded for the benefit of the ideal student his own conception of man—above all, Hispanic man—with a compensatory satisfaction that must have aided the serener flow of a poetry in the eidetic genre of Bello.

Of Juan de Mairena, Machado informs us in his introduction to the *Apocryphal Songbook* that he was a poet, philosopher, and rhetorician, born in Seville in 1865 and buried in Casariego de Tapia in 1909. He wrote, Machado tells us, a "Life of Abel Martín," an "Ars Poetica," a collection of verse called "Mechanical Couplets," and a treatise of metaphysics entitled "The Seven Reverses": thus Machado deploys his fictive persona to function as a real identity for a plurality of interests. In the first edition of the aphorisms and epigrams of Mairena, José Machado, the brother of the poet, includes an ink drawing of the apocryphal professor, presenting to the world an angular face, gaunt of cheek, with abundant hair and a small, feminine mouth. There are portraits of the youthful Machado which bear striking resemblance to it; and it can hardly be doubted that the poet's brother intended to suggest thereby a consanguinity with Mairena that, to a certain degree, he also shared.

We know, through Mairena's own words, of at least two childhood episodes, also recorded by Machado in his unpublished notebooks in the form of personal reminiscences, though it would be hard to determine from the facts which of his two doubles they involve. According to Mairena, the most important incident in his life—one which may well have prefigured certain aspects of his character and destiny—is the following: "While still just a boy, I was out walking one day with my mother, with a stick of sugarcane in my hand. It was in Seville, in the vanished days of a Christmas. Not far from me walked another mother with another child, also holding fast to a stalk of sugar-cane. I was quite certain that mine was the largest—absolutely convinced of it! Nevertheless, I turned to my mother and I asked—as children will do, to confirm even their own firsthand evidence: 'Mine's the biggest, isn't it?' 'No, child,' my mother answered me, 'have you no eyes in your head?' I have been asking myself that question all the rest of my life."

Machado's personal version shows certain discrepancies of detail—as, for example, the fact that it was his grandmother and not his mother who accompanied him on that occasion. "It seems hardly possible," the poet says of the above episode, "that such a trivial happening could have exerted so powerful an influence on my life. Whatever I am today, the good and the bad together, whatever remains of failure or reflection, I attribute to my memory of the sugarcane." Here, the autobiographical datum serves to illuminate the degree to which the identity of the fictive personage and his creator intermingle—a curious kind of intellectual symbiosis welling up from the depths of a childhood, in a literary re-creation, to achieve what Unamuno once called speaking of the protagonists in a novel, a "second-class life."

There are other oblique testimonies to this double life of Machado-Mairena, which, when examined in the light of the personality of Mairena, prove to be little more than aspects of the habitual life of the poet, Machado—for example, his alleged deafness, his irascibility, his typically Machadian greatcoat. Mairena was, in his own words, "intellectually hard of hearing" in the sense that he was slow to reply to questions addressed to him and, on at least one occasion, answered not at all—lost, as he later explains, in "absent-mindedness, trance, self-absorption," and the "practice of submitting to pestilential reflection all matters put to him before venturing an answer." There is also on record an occasion when Mairena, in the interests of a friend genuinely afflicted with this misfortune, resolved to simulate deafness whenever conversing with him, "with the aim," as he said, "of preserving the good man's illusion that there was at least one of his companions in misfortune who had achieved some degree of distinction."

Elsewhere, Machado informs us that "Mairena was one of the most inflammable people in the world," and then proceeds to illustrate with an example that may well have come from the arsenal of his own professional experience with those provincial schools where he was fated to pass the greater part of his lifetime. He was, so he tells us, visited once by the irate parent of a student who complained loudly, not of the injustice of his son's failing grade, but of the superficiality of the examination given. He received an acid answer from Mairena. The scene unfolds in this fashion: "'Do you mean to tell me you can flunk a student by just looking at him?' the visitor asked, flinging his arms wide in a crude attempt at ironical incredulity. Mairena, red with anger and crashing his pointer down on his desk, replied: 'I mean to tell you I have only to look at his father!'"

Similarly, the episode of Mairena's greatcoat bears directly on that "homeliest of sartorial embellishments" to which Machado refers in his personal self-portrait. It was the custom of his apocryphal double, we learn, on the bitterest winter days to wear a coarse outer garment which he used to call his "Catalan Vengeance," because the fabric was of a species milled in Catalonia that weights the wearer without warming him. "'The peculiarity of this greatcoat,' Mairena told his students, 'is that when brushed it whisks up more dust than it ever whisks away, because a natural avidity for dust particles has rendered the nap overly absorbent, and a dusty deposit was long ago packed into the weave of the fibre itself.'" It was also an idiosyncracy of Mairena's to run his watch behind time; and village wits had something to say on the score in the local gossip columns: "Doubtless, it was his way of solving the difficult problem of living in the past and meeting his current engagements punctually when necessary. Still, it must have been rather disconcerning to hear twelve strike in the still of the night, consult one's watch, and exclaim: 'What a bother! Twelve already!' But later to add with a smile: 'But it's twelve o'clock yesterday by my watch!'" A naturally modest soul, on the occasion when his admirers proposed to erect a monument to his memory, he advised the students who had raised the necessary funds to distribute them equally among the local sewer-wardens.

Officially, Mairena taught gymnastics in the local public school; his classes in rhetoric were, strictly speaking, outside the province of his assigned duties—marginal to the curriculum and dimly viewed by his disapproving colleagues. Similarly, Machado taught French in public high schools, along prescribed routines that could have offered him scant gratification, compelled as he was to teach without deviation and with little hope of altering his mode of living. Later, it is true, he was reassigned to teach Spanish literature, a subject more in keeping with his intellectual interests; but his latent vocation, which he continued to deepen and augment, remained philosophy. As has already been noted, Machado was not permitted to exercise this cherished competency, and in all probability he would have felt a certain diffidence about philosophizing "with magisterial solemnity."

The fact goes far toward explaining the captious and facetious tone with which the apocryphal professor characteristically philosophizes in *Juan de Mairena*, or simulates philosophy, or occasionally lampoons the philosophers by whose aid, carrying his gospel to the uncouth, he achieved passing compensation. On the other hand, Mairena's notorious aversion to gymnastics is plainly analogous to Machado's views on the teaching of French to provincial students wholly apathetic to the language. Unfortunately, there is little evidence today of his actual pedagogical practices (some class notes on Spanish literature of slight value), and his students do not seem to have preserved any notable impression of their mentor. It is no disservice to his memory to recall that as a teacher Machado was ill-suited to the curricular stereotypes to which he was expected to conform.

In return for his habitual reticence and assorted inhibitions, Machado—never a man to bask in the glare of popular scrutiny or make a public spectacle of himself—devoted himself to the creation of a Mairena busy with public lectures: a bustling disseminator of ideas and the apostle of a private pedagogical program. According to his "biographer," the rhetorical gymnast from Seville lectured copiously in every hamlet and township of Andalusia. Two fragments of his lectures have been preserved: "The Sermon at Rute," and another speech given at Chipiona, later rebaptized "The Sermon at Chipiona." In the former, Mairena ventures a prediction concerning the future of communism and Russia—a highly erroneous one, as it turns out, proving once more the idleness of prophets who undertake to prophesy on sociopolitical matters. As Mairena then saw things, the Russians would never submit to Marxist-Leninism, owing to the character of their historic Christianity, which, said Mairena, would soon transform Russian communism into a species of autocratic religiosity similar to the orthodox state-Church of an earier era. History has demonstrated the fallacy of this view; and there can be little doubt that the echo of his words would have sounded weirdly irrelevant in his own ears in years to come. The "Sermon at Chipiona" takes Christ and Plato for its theme, and is an effort in a lighter vein to link the doctrine of essences with Christian idealism.

There are times when one senses in Mairena a positive disdain for Antonio Machado; and in the columns of an apocryphal news sheet—"The Chipiona Beacon"—he actually went so far as to maintain that the poet was no better than a poetaster—"a Sevillian poetaster who had strayed into the Sorian uplands." Thus, the complex personality of Machado gives repeated expression to his self-doubt and existential dissatisfaction, projecting his loneliness upon an "other" of distinctly gregarious and volatile habits—an identity, unlike himself, in harmony with the here and now—with the friends, admirers, discipleship, public fame which were never vouchsafed to the poet. Between Juan de Mairena—sophist, gymnast, and mediator charged with the zeal of social pedagogy—and the reclusive poet—half forgotten in the solitude of the provinces—the compensatory byplay is sufficiently subtle to constitute a kind of martyrdom.

Mairena tells us that he came upon Henri Bergson in the last years of his life. If so, it was an epoch—*circa* 1908—in which the Neo-Kantian school of Marburg dominated virtually the whole European philosophical orbit, when a bid for the philosophy of Bergson would have needed more than ordinary professorial daring. Since Mairena died in 1909, according to Machado, his Mairenian "other" may be expected to embody intellectual interests typical of the poet up to this date. However, there is a posthumous resurgence of Mairena which follows still another curiously analogical pattern: "*If* Mairena were still alive, he *would have thought* thus and such on these matters"—which means in effect that we have now to deal with two superimposed Mairenas: a Mairena who *was,* still extant in the evidence of his writings, and a Mairena who *might have been,* cherished in Machado's memory of his writings.

However, this is not the place to enlarge on further intrications and admixtures. What needs to be said is that the death of Mairena coincides with a rising cycle of philosophical influence to which Machado was highly attentive—namely, existentialism. Supposedly Machado was acquainted with the work of Heidegger through French translations, and sensed the affinity between the new theoretical vision and his own poetry pierced by existential insights. He did not, however, devote himself to the systematic pursuit of a changing dialectic. A disciple of the Institución Libre de Enseñanza, he remains essentially the Kantian or Hegelian idealist, seeking to preserve in his "other" an image basically faithful to his educational tradition, and to secure its function as expositor of that ideology of '98 he was already leaving behind him in the years of the Spanish Civil War. In the social pedagogy scattered throughout the *Epigrams, Maxims, Memoranda, and Memoirs of Juan de Mairena,* Machado still declares for the shibboleths of '98 and retains its institutional stamp—the concern for the ethic and character of Spain, the political and historical self-criticism, the folkloric zeal, the Rousseauesque vision of nature and the praise of the natural man, the emphasis on the dignity of labor, and the rest of it.

Only in the posthumous Mairena and the notes and memories of Juan de Mairena written between 1937 and 1939 do we find an attempt to reconcile the two ideologies which confronted each other in the poet's thinking at this time. His reading of Heidegger had in essence uncovered for him a theoretical instrument which approximated a poetic creation; and it is possible that, had Machado been granted a longer life, we may have well witnessed, through the mediation of the Spanish poets—his beloved Jorge Manrique not excluded—a triumph of vision similar to that effected by the union of Heidegger and Hölderlin: the word that reveals the world to the man in this world (*Dasein in der Welt*) and the transcendency that bestows upon men an understanding of the "very waters of life itself," in Saint Teresa's phrase. Machado himself intimates nothing less, through the person of his double: "All that was Bergsonian in Mairena was poised to penetrate the new philosophy and espouse it with a whole heart."

What impressed Machado, shaking his imagination like a sudden confirmation of his own profoundest surmise, was the fact that Heidegger had rooted the whole of his ontology in the domain of the unexceptional man—the man in the street—grounding his comprehension of being in the truths of his most trivial experiences. In his brief but concentrated appraisal of the Heideggerian position, the "posthumous" Mairena remarks that the ordinary Spanish layman was more attuned to the life and the insights of existentialism than his European neighbors, because of his long ethical and religious preoccupation with the themes of temporality, anguish, and death. It was Heidegger's triumph to force man's resurgence out of that trivial daily life where the *Dasein* slumbers under the shell of Everyman—out of all that is spurious in gregarious man, and to bring him to ontological anguish. It is the same anguished being, born out of existential intuition of his Nothingness, that Unamuno knew; and Machado similarly took occasion to point out that the poems of his youth were conceived under the shadow of that poison tree. "Can it be that we Spaniards were always Heideggerians without ever realizing it?" Mairena asks. "Who is to say," he continues in his conclusion to the gloss on Heidegger, "what order of transcendency might not follow from a philosophy which, to the timeless question of metaphysics, 'What is Being?' replies: 'Search for it in human existence . . . The only door to Being lies in the venture of man's existence—man's being in the world and man's being in time.' It is this profoundly lyrical intimation which will draw the poets to the philosophy of Heidegger like butterflies to the sun." Time has proved him right.

Later, the disaster of his death revealed the further fact that, in drafting some autobiographical notes for Gerardo Diego's *Anthology* in 1931, Machado had declared in his own person: "All poets, consciously or unconsciously, predicate an existentialist metaphysics in their assumption that Time has an absolute value in itself"; and: "All that the poet sings, is a revelation of Being to consciousness." Here again is a clearly Heideggerian meeting of minds. If further proof is wanting, we may appeal to an apothegm from Juan de Mairena for the last word: "The day may yet come when the poets will change places with the philosophers. The poets will sing of their wonderment in the presence of the great metaphysical adventure . . . and the philosophers, pondering like poets the *fugit irreparabile tempus,* will gradually muffle their viols with veils. And out of that romantic deviation, an existentialist metaphysics will emerge rooted deeply in Time; something, in fact, more poetical than philosophical in character. For the philosophers will speak to us of our anguish, the essentially poetical anguish of Being, face to face with non-Being, while the poets will appear drunken with radiance, reeling under the old Eleatic superlatives. Thus poet and philosopher will confront each other, no longer enemies, each carrying forward the great labor where it is relinquished by the other."

SEGUNDO SERRANO PONCELA

Universidad Central de Venezuela, Caracas

Translated by Ben Belitt

Translator's Preface

Tradition has reserved this space for the translator's apology for his translation. Machadians will not have to be informed of the hazards of translating either the prose of *Juan de Mairena* or the lyrics of the *Apocryphal Songbooks;* and apology is lost upon those who assume that Machado, a master of the "middle style," and a conspicuous adversary of the baroque, is always leathery, open, and linear, "like the landscapes of Castile." A. Sańchez Barbudo, in his tour de force of clarification, *The Thought of Antonio Machado,* * takes pains to remind the casual reader of the "enigmatic" and "disconcerting" character of the *Apocryphal Songbooks* and the "obscurity of the philosophical writings." Similarly, the author of *The World and the Work of Antonio Machado,* † whose essay launches this translation for American readers, is concerned with the "mirror play," the "screens," the "apocryphal compensations," and the "hermetic" aspects of the later Machado. All present problems for the translator which may well prove insuperable.

In another sense, however, it has always been the translator's task to devise an "apocryphal life" for a text which can have no second being apart from the linguistic and imaginative processes intrinsic to its original containment of experience. "The only living language," Mairena somewhere remarks, "is the language in which we think and have our being. We are given only one . . . we must content ourselves with the surfaces, grammatical and literary, of all the others." The "Otherness" with which Mairena, Martín, and Machado are all severally preoccupied and which

---

* See note p. xi.

† Segundo Serrano Poncela, *Antonio Machado: Su mundo y su obra* (Buenos Aires: Editorial Losado, S.A., 1954).

the translator presumably shares—which "persists and suffices for itself" and "will submit to no elimination"—has its absolute in the work of art from which translation begins. Here, it would seem, art has achieved what logic and contemplation—least of all, translation!—could not: the unique engagement of language and sensibility in an artifact which, once realized, remains "immutable, anchored forever, as it were, in the river of Heraclitus"; for which the only mode of existence is the mode of its original being.

However, as Machado also reminds us, "we live in an essentially apocryphal world, a cosmos or poem of our own thinking, ordered and structured on undemonstrable suppositions"; and it is here that the translator may find both the premise of his vocation and the necessary autonomy of his commitment. In *Juan de Mairena,* where the spectrum of "Otherness" is already multiple, and the screens, masks, doubles, and transpositions threaten the world of the poet with that Nothingness which Martín preëmpted for his God, the translator has a special labor of fidelity. He must play "Class Listener," like Mairena's "*oyente,*" to the many voices of Machado as they have already shaped the intonation of his prose style: the magisterial mode of the schoolteacher, smelling faintly of chalk and the morning *tertulia;* the sententious and hortatory inflection of the moralist, with its blend of intimacy and asperity; the colloquial turns which are there because the speaker, a man of gregarious habits, has declared for a literature that is "spoken" rather than "written"; the poet concerned with enigma, and the philosopher concerned with ideality, turning bafflement into irony and aphorism into misgiving. These are rhetorical specifics for the literature of a wry and hermetic intelligence; these are linguistic particulars for that "heterogeneity of Being" which the poet enacts and the translator simulates.

The Appendix of poems from the *Apocryphal Songbooks* (in a sequence which is mine, not Machado's) are another matter, differing in the mode of their translation as the exigencies of poetry differ from prose. Here the attempt has been to communicate the power and density of the originals by equivalent facts of *form,* in a matrix of English which at times transposes the Spanish effects directly, and at other times builds on the thrust of English prosody, as a collateral "fact of form." The hope is to suggest by this means the internality of Machado's lyricism—its hermetic integrity, if you wish; not, however, in the manner of the hermit crab who backs himself into the shell of larger crustaceans, but by parallel acts of self-containment. Thus, much of "The Death of Abel Martín" reproduces a line-for-line profile of the original, with incidental transpositions of content and prosody; and the English of "Two Songs" might be said literally to follow *after* the Spanish of Antonio Machado to achieve a monolithic entirety of song by processes inherent to English. Here, emendation and paraphrase are more frequent, especially in the "untranslatable" locutions of a syntax which is fluid in Spanish and polyglot in English; but in each instance I have sought to render the pulls of meaning and melody organically comparable.

As editor, I also have to account for the diminished equivalence of a text which, in its original version, runs to 324 pages, as published by Espasa-Calpe in Madrid in 1936. One hopes, of course, for a distillation and not a mutilation of the essential Machado, preserving the total balance of his preoccupations as apocryphal Juan—the poetics, metaphysics, politics (in the conceptual sense), pedagogy, dialectic, rhetoric, theology, and *belles-lettres;* the passion for *otredad* ("Otherness"), *la nada* ("Nothingness"—and a Spaniard's Nothingness is like nobody else's), *heterogeneidad* ("heterogeneity"), *el Ser* ("Being"); and assorted ironical entertainments. I have omitted all later emendations, pendants, and appendices, largely patriotic and political, of the "posthumous" Mairena, which follow the 1936 canon, and the extended poetics attached to the *cancioneros* of Martín and Mairena, which should some day be translated intact. The complexity and sweep of the latter, as Barbudo has ably demonstrated, are indisputable; but for that very reason, their effect in the present volume would be to tilt the balance of masks, identities, screens, and impersonations, and to misplace the gravity of that apocryphal world which, in *Juan de Mairena,* is not encompassed but suspended. The result, I am satisfied, is a treasury of the mind and sensibility of a major imaginative intelligence, cut to the sequences and the fifty chapters of the original and preserving their total ensemble.

In the guise of poet, immersed in the labor of translating and construing a creative phenomenon and viewing it from the stance of ontological criticism, I should like to venture an afterthought. Recent scholarship has focused sedulously on the philosophical texture of Machado's accomplishment, and for very good reason: it *is* substantively philosophical in both its effects and its sources, and its ambiguities require the glosses of the historian of ideas. That a philosopher-poet who aims at "maximizing temporality" should himself be volatilized in time in the end—in depth as well as in historical extension—is by no means surprising; and with Machado, there is reason to probe for conceptual and metaphysical consequences. The area has been abundantly delved by Barbudo, Poncela, Aranguren, Bellé, de Torre, and others, and the affinities with Heidegger, Bergson, Jaspers, Unamuno, the early phenomenologists and the later existentialists, are available to connoisseurs of letters and ideas.

It may be time again to view the identical circumstance "poetically," as Machado himself preferred to view both the meanings and the modality of philosophy—from Kant's dove and Heraclitus' river (and Archimedes' lever?) to the culminating refinements of Heideggerian "*Sorge.*" Seen from this vantage point, it is the apocryphal, rather than the "existential," datum which becomes primary: all the modes of simulation and dissimulation by which a poet accommodates himself to his own strangeness and displaces the world with his being. Put it another way: the daimon of the Apocrypha points to Creation, and the angel of Existenz points to Being, both in the spirit of Mairena's benevolent diabolism: "You have excellent parents who deserve your respect and affection: why not go on to invent better?"

So viewed—as invention rather than meditation—it is Kierkegaard, rather than Heidegger or Bergson, who emerges as the apocryphal "familiar" of Antonio Machado. The affinities, I dare say, are analogical rather than demonstrable—a kinship of identities, rather than a collation of conceptual thought. Yet they are there, just as the invention present in the minds of two discrete intelligences, saturated with the immanence of things to come but widely separated in space, might simultaneously produce the incandescent bulb or the second law of thermodynamics. There comes to mind, first of all, the fact of their mutual compulsion for the pseudonymous life—in the sense that Poncela insists it should apply here: Machado-Mairena-Martín, on the one hand, and Kierkegaard on the other in the guise of the Seducer, or the Editor presiding over the simulated identities of the "A" of *Either* and the "B" of *Or,* and signing himself "Victor Eremita" (as in "hermetic"). Like Machado, the editorial Eremita is preoccupied with a tactic of doubleness and systematic hoax, and its confessional revelations of being: "In the confessional, the priest is separated from the penitent by a screen; he does not see, he only hears. Gradually, as he listens, he constructs an outward appearance which corresponds to the voice he hears. Consequently, he experiences no contradiction. It is otherwise, however, when you hear and see at the same time and yet perceive a screen between yourself and the speaker." Like Machado, too, Kierkegaard, caught in the anguish of the apocryphal life, is compelled to concede at last: "One author seems to be enclosed in another, like the parts of a Chinese puzzle-box . . . The dominant mood of A's preface in a manner betrays the poet. It seems as if A had actually become afraid of his poem, as if it continued to terrify him, like a troubled dream when it is told."

It is precisely at this point that the nuances begin to multiply. If Machado has his brandy bottle and his greatcoat to fortify the inner and outer man of his professor and cloak the "memoranda, epigrams, maxims, *et cetera*" of a philosopher *manqué,* Kierkegaard has his apocryphal escritoire, purchased at second hand and honeycombed with secret recesses, which, at a lucky hatchet blow, spills out the manuscript pages of *Either/Or.* Nor is it surprising that, in one instance, the final stroke of the hatchet breaks open the box of the erotic, to reveal the "Diary of a Seducer"; and, in the second instance, that Machado focuses on Don Juan, in all his mutations, as "hero of the Christian temper," on the clothed and unclothed Maja, Jack the Ripper as a travesty of deprived paternity, a tragicomedy by Mairena called *The Grand Climacteric,* the randy diabolism of Espronceda, and a schoolboy's parody of dialectic on the theme of "Nudity and Liberty, Properly Understood."

The relation of the erotic to the apocryphal life in each instance is somber and teasing, and merits its fair share of illumination, along with Machado's affinities with the existentialists, as modes of being and compensation. Kierkegaard's broken engagement to Regina and the elegiac pathos of Machado as lifelong mourner, widower, and solitary are equally germane to the poetry of deprival and the philosophy of "ontological anguish." Certainly the theme of anguish—specifically, poetic anguish—is constant throughout the *Diapsalmata ad se ipsum* of Kierkegaard: "A critic resembles a poet to a hair, he only lacks the anguish of poets and the music on his lips. I tell you, I would rather be a swineherd understood by the swine, than a poet misunderstood by men." And the *lacrimae rerum* of Machado are similarly present in Kierkegaard, with an identical hermetic inflection: "I say of my sorrow what the Englishman says of his house: My sorrow is my castle." So, too, are the satanism of Don Juan and the Donjuanesque; the primacy of the folkloric; "the courage to doubt everything"; the faith in the clairvoyance of children and the indelible persistence of their memory; the themes of dread, futurity, and the mystery of identity ("One ought to be a mystery not only to others, but also to oneself."); the incompatibility of causes and effects, questions and answers; the preoccupation with Shakespeare, God, the classics, the Old Testament; apocalyptical presentiments of earthquake, waterspouts, judgment, death, and non-Being. Indeed, the shared preoccupations of Kierkegaard and Machado are circumstantial enough to constitute a "doubleness" which is no longer the invention of a conspiratorial intelligence, but a clue to our contemporaneity and that "essentially apocryphal" character of the world which, in Machado's view, produced the "cosmos or poem of our thinking."

In that "poem," Machado does not stand alone among his countrymen: the effect of his premise is rather to turn the whole literature of Europe into a parable of avid apocryphal quest. In the vanguard—or so Machado would have us believe—comes his beloved Cervantes in the guise of Quijote–Sancho Panza: a "twinned series of figures, real and hallucinatory . . . two integral, complementary consciousnesses, conversing and forging ahead." And moving into our own century, there follows an array of animal and human *Doppelgänger* whose passion for Otherness, heterogeneity, and the apocryphal has left its abiding mark on the literature of our epoch. Federico García Lorca readily comes to mind, in the masks of Camborio, Sanchez Mejías, *gitano legítimo,* a quartet of saints and a repertory of plays, with his child's outcry: "¡Qué raro que me llame Federico!" ("How odd to be called Federico!"); then Valle-Inclán, in the ruff and derring-do of Marques de Bradomín, "el mas admirable de los Don Juanes: feo, católico, y sentimental" ("the most admirable of the Don Juans: ugly, Catholic, and sentimental"), pursuing his doubleness in its erotic and seasonal guises; Rimbaud as *Vierge Folle* and *L'Époux Infernal* peering full face from a profile of Verlaine, like a portrait by Picasso, and calling to his counterfeits: "Duval, Dufour, Armand, Maurice, que sais-je? . . . A chaque être plusières autres vies me semblaient dues" ("Duval, Dufour, Armand, Maurice, what am I?. . . To each, I thought, many other lives had been given."); Rilke as Cornet Christopher, Knight of the Bilderbuch, and "other self" of Malte Laurids Brigge: "Sie werden sich hundert neue Namen geben und einander alle wieder abnehmen, leise, wie man einen Ohrring abnimmt." ("They will give each other a hundred new names and take them away as lightly as one takes off an earring."); Mallarmé as des Esseintes: "Nous fûmes deux, je le mantiens!" ("I insist, we were two!"); Eliot as J. Alfred Prufrock: "No, I am not Prince Hamlet, nor was meant to be / Am an attendant lord . . ."); Yeats in the hermetic panoply of the Mask and the Image, stalking the daimon of his Anti-Self on the Path of the Chameleon:

> I, that my native scenery might find imaginary inhabitants, half-planned a new method and a new culture. My mind began drifting vaguely toward that doctrine of "the mask" which has convinced me that every passionate man . . . is, as it were, linked to another age, historical or imaginary, where alone he finds images that rouse his energy. . . . Image called up image

> in an endless procession, and I could not always choose among them with any confidence; and when I did choose, the image lost its intensity, or changed into some other image . . . I was lost in that region a cabalistic manuscript . . . had warned me of; astray upon the Path of the Chameleon, upon *Hodos Chameleontos.*

Thus, between Greek and Irish, Yeats, too, evokes the *Nada* of Machado and suggests its anguish.

Last of all, on his own soil, I would summon Juan Ramón Jiménez in the guise of the celebrated donkey of Moguer. Smelling deceptively of sweet marjoram and eating pomegranate kernels, he is actually a cosmology, like the tortoises of China or the Leviathan of the Hebrews, charged with the ambiguity of a myth and the immediacy of a totem animal. Summoned into being with all the tender variations of his name—Platero! Plateron! Platerillo! Platerete!—he takes shape in a pastoral haze, in a landscape where even the "flowering ground appears dreamlike, a strange lace, primitive, beautiful," drinking the sugary flesh of watermelons, at once vegetal and incarnate, fabulous and actual, secular and paschal, lyrical and irreducible. At his side, *within* him as well as *upon* him, goes the image of a poet not unlike Machado in temperament, "dressed in mourning, with my beard cut like a Nazarene's and my narrow-brimmed hat," among festivals and fast days, like a genius of uncommitted pathos. These, then, are the "apocrypha" of a century which has in every decade sent its poets back to the *Nada,* as Mairena sends the student to the blackboard, to trace on the void, in erasable chalk, improvisations of assertion and selfhood, in a timeless comedy of transcendence.

A final paragraph of acknowledgment: to Dr. Luis Monguió, chiefly, of the Department of Spanish and Portuguese, University of California, Berkeley, for a detailed scrutiny of the first draft and a subsequent clarification that would merit the epithet of collaborative, if the translation itself were less vulnerable; to August Frugé, Director of the University of California Press, for many favors of consideration and encouragement; to Bennington College, for a Huber Fund Grant which made possible my sojourn at the University of California; to the YMHA-Bollingen Foundation for their commission to translate the poems of the *Apocryphal Songbooks* and permission to include them in this volume; and to *Poetry* (Chicago) for the right to reprint them.

BEN BELITT

Bennington College, 1963
Bennington, Vermont

Juan de Mairena

TALKS WITH HIS STUDENTS

I

℄ Truth's truth—Agamemnon's word or his swineherd's— never mind whose!
AGAMEMNON: True enough!
SWINEHERD: I'm not convinced . . .

℄ *Mairena in his class in poetry and rhetoric*

"Mr. Perez, go to the board and write: 'The quotidian events which occur on the highways and byways.' "

The student writes as dictated.

"Now render that poetically."

The student thinks for a moment, and writes: "What goes on in the streets."

MAIRENA: Not bad!

℄ Day by day, gentlemen, literature is becoming more written and less spoken. As a result, day by day, writing deteriorates: our prose, for all its propriety, is frigid and graceless, and our oratory a rehash of the written word, under which the spoken word has been all but smothered. Scratch an orator these days and you will find all the blotches and blottings of the journalist. The important thing is to speak well: briskly, logically, and resourcefully. The rest will take care of itself.

ℭ *On the difficulties of dialogue*

"Our writers of comedy will always fall short of the sparkle and pace of true theater without a careful study of the dialectics of humor." This observation of Juan de Mairena's is accompanied by a formula for dialogue in which one of the two participants is always disposed to agree, with loud cries of "Certainly! Certainly!" while the other answers, like clockwork: "What's so certain? What's so certain?" In this specimen of dialogue, the former grants all the answers without ever troubling to listen and the latter reverses himself the moment his partner concurs.

ℭ *Concerning truth*

Gentlemen, Mairena observed to his students of rhetoric, man's truth begins where his absurdities end. But man's folly is inexhaustible. Put it another way: orators are born; poets are made by the grace of God.

ℭ The common tendency of man is to accept the expedient as truth: Therefore humbug is general. I offer this in behalf of those contemplating a political career. Bear in mind, however, that the "common" lot of man embraces only what is "common" to his species as predator: what is specifically human is man's conviction of death. Never assume that your task as rhetoricians is to betray man to his own appetites, for man's passion for truth is such that he will welcome the bitterest of all postulates so long as it strikes him as true.

ℭ Blasphemy is part and parcel of all popular religion. Beware of the community in which blasphemy does not exist: underneath, atheism runs rampant. Proscribe it with punitive laws as drastic as you please and you will poison the heart of a people and turn their dialogue with divinity into a fraud. Will the God who reads all human hearts allow Himself to be so swindled? He would sooner forgive the professed heretic—never doubt it!—than the latent desecration of the hypocrite who sins in his soul—or, more hypocritically still, subverts his blasphemy into prayer.

ℭ Blasphemy is more than mere "folklore," as my teacher Abel Martín used to maintain. In any duly constituted faculty of theology, a chair of blasphemy—in preparation for the doctorate, of course—would be indispensable: occupied by the Devil himself, if possible.

ℭ "Develop that theme a little, Mr. Rodríguez."

"Well," says Rodríguez in a fine burst of oratory, "in a Christian republic—that is to say, a community committed to liberalism and democracy—the Devil would be entitled to citizenship like anyone else—he should be forced to abide by the laws, charged with certain duties, and endowed with certain rights—above all, the specifically demoniacal right to voice his own thoughts. Let the Devil speak up as a devil: give him the floor, gentlemen. Never fear: the Devil will never be right (tiene razón), but he will always be handy with reasons (tiene razones). Hear him out to the end."

ℭ Wherever learning breeds specialists, the sum of human culture is enhanced thereby. That is the illusion and consolation of specialists. What is generally known by everybody, on the other hand, is the province of nobody!

ℭ It is possible for every human soul, Mairena once quoted his teacher, to be total in intimacy—lyrically speaking, a monad without windows or doors, a melody sung to the self and heard by a self deaf and indifferent to all other melodies, however like or unlike, produced by all other souls. The conductor's baton would obviously be useless here. Rather, we would have to postulate Leibnitz's lofty hypothesis of a pre-established harmony, with a great ear attuned to a great symphony. Why not, for that matter, a great bedlam?

☾ As an annihilating argument against all skeptics, it is commonly urged: Those who deny the existence of the truth postulate the truth of their denial and plainly contradict themselves. This doughty argument has, however, never really convinced skeptics. The whole piquancy of skepticism lies in the fact that arguments never convince. And skeptics are not concerned about convincing others.

☾ "Either God exists or He does not exist! Affirm it or deny it as you please, when the chips are down—but never *doubt* it."
"That's what *you* think!"

☾ "An existing God," my teacher used to say, "what a dreadful possibility! God save us from the likes of Him!"

II

℄ We have never taken kindly, Juan de Mairena once remarked, to the sound of the word bourgeois. Not even today, when the bourgeoisie—after a century and a half of happy predominance—has fought off the fiercest and most sedulous attackers, buckler on forearm, would one venture to call oneself bourgeois. Nevertheless, the bourgeoisie of this world, with their liberalism, their individualism, their capitalist organization, their positive science, their industrial, technological, and mechanical advances—along with other virtues, like socialism, that intrinsically bourgeois invention—is hardly so despicable a class that Monsieur Jourdain need groan with the shame of it; he might even prefer it, at times, to his chimerical gentry.

℄ Never (Nunca), nothingness (Nada), nobody (Nadie). Three terrible words: above all, the last. Nobody is the personification of Nothingness. Nevertheless, man has taken up the burden of these words and is even losing his fear of them. Don Nadie! Don José María Nadie! His Excellency Lord Nadie! "Imagine it totally," Mairena cautioned his students, "get used to the sound of it. As an exercise for poets, I can think of nothing more edifying. That will be all."

℄ Mairena once told his class in rhetoric: The word "representation," which has vitiated all theories of knowledge, involves a number of ambiguities that may well prove dismal for poets. Things are either present or absent to the consciousness; but it is no easy matter to determine what is represented in the consciousness, and nobody has actually done so. And even if we could concede that consciousness offers something like a mirror in which images more or less equivalent to things in themselves are reflected, we would always have to inquire: and how does consciousness itself perceive the images reflected in its mirror? For the image cast on a mirror poses a problem of perception equal to that of the object as much. We obviously tend to attribute to the mirror of man's consciousness a miraculous power of awareness and assume that *an image in the consciousness is equivalent to the consciousness of an image.* Thus, one begs the eternal problem posed by the data of common sense: that of the absolute heterogeneity of conscious acts in relation to objects of sense.

I invite all would-be poets and imaginative artists to mull the matter over. As such, you will always have to deal with the presence or the absence of things; never with imitation, translations, or representations.

℄ "Our love of God," Spinoza somewhere remarks, "is a part of the love with which God loves Himself." "How God must have chortled," my teacher observed, "over this nimble and ingenuous *reductio ad absurdum* of the concept of love!" Our greatest philosophers have always been jugglers of divinity.

℄ From the One to the Other is the great theme of metaphysics. The whole travail of human reason has been to liquidate the second of the two terms. The Other does not exist: that is rational faith, the incurable conviction of all human reason. Identity = reality: as if, when all is said and done, all had to be, necessarily and absolutely, *one and the same.* But the Other will never submit to such elimination: it persists and it suffices for itself; it is the hard bone on which reason fastens its teeth and all but gnaws them away. Abel Martín, in the faith of poetry, which is no less human than the rational kind, believed in the Other, in the "Essential Heterogeneity of Being," the incurable Otherness, so to speak, underlying the life of the One.

℄ *Class jotting*

MAIRENA: Mr. Martínez, go to the board and write

The olden blades of a glorious day . . .

Martínez complies.

MAIRENA: Now to what day do you think the poet is alluding?

MARTÍNEZ: The day in which the blades no longer were olden.

III

¶ *On politics*

In Spain—let us remember—political action of a progressive character has always tended to be feeble, because it has lacked true originality; it has dealt in mere mimicry, to draw out the wrath of reactionaries. One might go on to point out that the only gambit which has functioned with any sort of energy or precision in our social machine is the reactionary one. Politicians with a mind to the future had better take note of the reaction-in-depth that follows every advance-on-the-surface in Spain. Our so-called solons of the left—a frivolous lot, on the whole, be it said—have rarely estimated, in discharging the rifle fire of their futurist rhetoric, the recoil of the rifle stock that is often, oddly enough, more jarring than the explosion itself.

¶ Liberty, gentlemen, Mairena points out to a student, is a metaphysical problem. However, there is always liberalism, an invention of the British, that great nation of sailors, ironists, and pugilists.

¶ Only the Britisher is capable of smiling at his adversary and congratulating him on the thump in the solar plexus that might well have finished him off. With one puffed eye and two broken ribs, the Englishman always seems to flatten his beefier but less battle-wary opponent, whose victories end in the rubbish heap. The British, in effect, have devised a decorum for fisticuffs, turning it into a kind of game, more or less violent, but always "cricket," in which one can win without arrogance or lose without undue remorse. Even in the most tragic of encounters which could never be confused with a game, man's ceaseless battle with the sea, the Britisher is the last to compromise with his fastidiousness. This is gospel truth. But where fighting is not the point, of what use are the British? All action, after all, is not polemical.

℄ The nineteenth century is an essentially quarrelsome one. The Darwinian struggle for life has been taken much too seriously. It seems to turn out this way: a fact is duly noted; then it is accepted as a fatality; and in the end it is turned into a flag. If it should become apparent some day that the fact was never a positive certainty, or was in fact an utter falsification, the flag, a little faded at the edges perhaps, would still flap in the breeze.

℄ "Man comes into the world with a chip on his shoulder. That is one of the essentially pagan dogmas of our time," Juan de Mairena once remarked to his charges.

"And what if Christ should return again, sir?"

"In that case," said Mairena, "all hell would break loose."

℄ Traditionalists should take to heart the arguments often used against them.

First, that if history, like time, is irreversible, there is no way of restoring the past.

Second, if there are aspects of history transcendent to time—eternal values, so to speak, not yet part of the past—it is pointless to talk of our ever retrieving them.

Third, if thus and so much dust tracks in thus and so much muck, the present ought not to be condemned and the past absolved.

Fourth, if we should turn back to all that dust, we would have to reckon again with all that muck.

Fifth, all regression, therefore, ends in a cave or an age of gold—which no one but Jean Jacques Rousseau ever believed in, and even he with moderation.

IV

¶ One expects that a public man, particularly a politician, will have public virtues, all of which can be summed up in the phrase: fidelity to his own mask. "My teacher used to say," Mairena told his students of sophistry, "that a public man who acquits himself badly in public is worse than a public woman who acquits herself badly in private. Joking aside," he added, "all political compromises end up in horse trading, a confusion of masks, amateur farces in which nobody knows his proper role. Take note of that: try, as far as possible—those of you who plan to be politicians—to fabricate your own masks; make them with your own hands, if you would frustrate others—your enemies or co-religionists—who would make them for you and clap them over your faces; and don't make them so rigidly, so opaquely and impenetrably, that you suffocate underneath them. Sooner or later you will have to show your true face, unmasked."

¶ Philosophy, viewed by the candid reason, is, as Hegel maintained, the world seen inside out. "Poetry, on the other hand," my teacher Abel Martín used to add, "is the precise opposite: the world seen, in the long run, right side out." That parenthetical "long run" shows the quizzical cast of my teacher's thinking: for to see things right side out, one must first have seen them topsy-turvy. Or vice versa.

¶ "Prose," Juan de Mairena told his students of literature, "ought never to be written too seriously. When humor is lost to prose—good humor or bad—the result is extemporaneous oratory or lyrical prose, so called: a sickening decoction!"

"But what about treatises on physics," a student protests, "what about tracts in biology . . . ?"

"Didactic prose is another matter. I suppose that has to be written in dead earnest. Nevertheless, a certain ironic flicker is never amiss. What would Dr. Laguna have lost if he had cut a few capers in the course of his *Dioscorides Anazarbeo** . . . ? We would think no less of him today: that he was learned, for his time, and that we should really get around to reading him some day."

☾ If some of you turn into critics of literature or the arts, try a little benevolence. There is no need to equate benevolence with a predilection for ruins or conformity with the inept, but rather a spirit of good will—in your case, an ardent desire to see the miracle of the beautiful accomplished. Only with this cut to his jib can the critic be fruitful. The malign critic who makes free with his petulance and melancholy is common enough in Spain, and finds nothing good enough for his taste. Truth to tell, he is not looking for excellence, and does not want it.

Not that malevolent critics have not coincided on occasion with the failures of an artistic intention. How often it happens that an inferior comedy is brutally flayed by a critic inferior to the comedy itself! "Do you follow me, Mr. Martínez?"

MARTÍNEZ: I believe so.

MAIRENA: Will you sum up my thought in a few words?

MAIRENA: Exactly.

MARTÍNEZ: Criticism is not synonymous with a sluggish liver.

☾ Nevertheless, malice, hatred, and envy have at times sharpened the perception of those critics who love to dwell on what is lacking in a work of art at the expense of all that is present. Malfunctions of the liver and stomach may even have collaborated with the fine frenzies of literature. But they have produced nothing of importance.

☾ "Does Balzac strike you as a good novelist?" a raw Athenaist from Chipiona once asked Juan de Mairena.

---

*Dioscorides was a Greek physician of the first century A.D. His *De Materia Medica* was translated into Spanish by Andrés de Laguna (1499–1560).

"To me he does."

"I don't know. To me he seems so insignificant that I've never even bothered to read him."

℄ *Juan de Mairena and his teacher, Abel Martín, tread on thin ice*

My teacher once told me: Karl Marx, gentlemen, was a German Jew who read Hegel Hebraically, with a materialist dialectic and a usurious view of the future. Justice for the multitudinous flock of mankind; the whole world for their pasture! With Marx, gentlemen, a barely Christianized Europe regressed to the Old Testament. But Russia survived—"Holy" Russia, whose spiritual roots are essentially evangelical. The exact interpretation of the fraternal sentiment of Christianity is specifically Russian. In a lull in the procreative Eros, which sought only survival in time from the Father to the Son, Christ proclaimed the brotherhood of men, loosed from the chains of blood kinship and terrestrial plenty: a triumph of the fraternal virtues over the patriarchal. The whole of Russian literature is charged with Christian spirituality. I can never conceive, gentlemen, of a Marxist Russia, since the true Russian begins where the Marxist leaves off. Proletariat of the world to the barricades, since nothing matters but the green pastures of mankind! That old shibboleth of seminal, Biblical humanity! Russia must never hear of it." (*Fragment of a discourse by Juan de Mairena known to his students as the "Sermon at Rute," because it was given in the auditorium there*)

V

ℂ *Mairena's classes*

Juan de Mairena had a way at times of admonishing his students in rather too elementary terms. Bear in mind, however, their extreme youth: they were mere children, hardly high-school graduates; and Mairena made a point of gathering the dullards in the first row of the class and addressing himself almost exclusively to them.

ℂ *Erudition*

The passion for truth is the noblest of all passions: agreed. Nevertheless, all is not gold that glitters. There is always with us a breed of scholars, investigators, and pedants who pursue the truth of persons and things in the hope of derogating them all, impelled by a passion for wrecking reputations and demolishing excellence.

I remember an erudite friend of mine who decided to take seriously one of our more daring class exercises: the one in which we set out to demonstrate that the *Dialogues* of Plato were actually manuscripts filched by Plato, not precisely from Socrates, who probably knew little about the graces of composition, but from Xantippe, his wife, whose good name history and criticism must some day vindicate. You remember our reasoning: "Plato's real name," so we said, "was Aristocles; but the Greeks of his day, who knew all about the philosopher's insignificance, and might as easily have called him Cephalo or Macrocephalo the old squarehead, chose to call him Plato (the broad-shouldered), a nickname more in keeping with a stadium athlete or a stevedore than with an intellectual luminary." Our explanation of Xantippe was equally logical: "Socrates' habit of roving the streets and bending the ear of the first man he met in the agora is clearly that of an exasperated husband turning his back on a household plagued by the intellectual superiority of his spouse." Of course, not all our arguments were as convincing to my friend. "That," he used to say, "will have to be gone into more thoroughly!" But he liked our proposition because it gave him a chance to kill two birds—eagles, at that—with one stone. In the end, he even produced a hypothesis of his own: that the condemnation of Socrates was another ruse of Xantippe's, who conspired with the judges to get rid of her good-for-nothing husband.

℄ *Poetic exercises on baroque themes*

"The classical mode," Mairena observes to his students, "involves the use of the substantive accompanied by a qualifying adjective. Thus, Homer alludes to the 'hollow ships,' which is less a description of a ship than a definition of one. The ship of Homer, however, sails substantially on, and will do so as long as Archimedean physics continues to obtain. The baroque adds nothing to the classical, but only jars its equilibrium a little, intensifying the role of the limiting adjective until it takes over the function of the noun itself. If we identify gold with its yellowness, and silver with its whiteness, the baroque finds nothing inappropriate in calling gold silver, so long as the silver is 'blond'; or silver gold, so long as the gold is 'hoary.' Do you follow me, Mr. Martínez?"

"I think I do."

"Go to the board and write

> Hoar gold I bring to you, not the blond silver

What does that mean, precisely?"

"That you're bringing me silver and not gold."

"Excellent! Now how does the line strike you?"

"Well . . . it's a fairly accurate hendecasyllable . . ."

"Is that all?"

"Well . . . that touch about calling silver gold and gold silver . . ."

"Now copy out the lines

> O ardent blond of the silver
> How you shame the hoar of the gold!

How does that strike you?"

"Well, that 'O ardent . . . silver' bit sounds pretty awful, and the 'How you shame . . .' even worse."

"True enough. But notice the conceptual richness of the lines and the intellectual gymnastics needed to construe them. 'The silver,' the poet is saying, 'so desirable when it is "blond" puts gold itself to shame, when it is "hoar," since silver, when it is gold, is of greater value than gold when it is silver—assuming, of course, that gold has a greater specific valuation than silver'—all that in two octosyllabic lines! Now I would like you to elaborate on our theme, in the baroque manner, for exactly four verses—not a line more."

Martínez, after a little thought, writes on the board

> Blond silver, raining gently down,
> is the hoar gold of the hurricane:
> the more the blondness in the ore,
> the less the summer in the rain.

"By summer, I mean harvest, plenty, abundance . . ."

"Exactly so, Mr. Martínez. There's a sharp lad!"

VI

◖ *Proverbs and admonitions of Mairena*

Men who are always coming back from something have never really gone anywhere. Granted, the going is hard; but as to coming back, no one ever really does that.

◖ Practice modesty: I recommend modesty, or rather a modest measure of pride, which is Christian as well as Castilian. The Castilians have a proverb: "No one is better than anybody else." I take it to mean that it is hard to outdistance all comers, because whatever a man comes to be worth, he can never hope to exceed his innate worth as a *man*.

◖ Avoid pulpits, platforms, stages, and pedestals. Keep to the hard ground; it is the only way you can judge your approximate stature as a man.

◖ As to homage, beware the monstrous irony of the Unknown Soldier, that poor prodigy dead on the field of battle who, should he raise his head by some miracle to tell us, "My name is Smith," would be shoveled under again with the cry: "Back to the void, Smith! This is no affair of yours!"

◖ Be on guard against me—do! I profess, in good faith, whatever seems best and most fruitful for your souls, using as a norm whatever seemed fruitful to mine. But that is a criterion open to many risks; I use it only because I know of no better one. I require only the little comradeship and respect that make possible a few hours of reciprocal communion. But don't take me too seriously. Remember: I am not at all certain of what I am saying, and though I intend your eventual education, I can't really believe that my own has gone much beyond yours. It isn't easy for me to teach you to speak and to write and to think effectively, since I am muddlement personified—a soul like a blotting pad, full of blotches, erasures, vacillations, misgivings. I've a devil inside me—not the dæmon of Socrates, but a kobold of sorts, who erases what I write down, if he pleases, and writes into the spaces the opposite of all he rubs out; who sometimes speaks through me, and I through him, when we are both not actually talking at once, in a chorus of opposites. There's a mishmash for you! I am not the teacher you would have chosen for yourselves with an eye to your future; you will learn from me only what you may have to unlearn for the rest of your lives: to mistrust yourselves utterly.

℄ There are people who never tire of adding to their stock of knowledge. Not a day passes—so they say—but they learn something new before bedtime! On the other hand, there are people who never tire of adding to their ignorance, who cannot sleep peacefully until they are sure they have totally unlearned something they thought they had mastered. "A equals A!" my teacher intoned as the sleep of eternity was darkening his vision. But later he added, in a voice no longer of this world: "Get that midge out of my eye, confound it!"

℄ The sculptor whom Zorilla brings out of the wings for a moment in his *Tenorio*—that Don Juan so often vilified by those who know nothing of the other Don Juans—is really a princely fellow. With what gusto he would have modeled a statue of Don Juan the "matador," as he puts it with incomparable ingenuity, and planted it in the thick of his hero's victims, on the highest pedestal of all!

To the ethical by way of the esthetic, as Juan de Mairena said, anticipating an illustrious countryman.*

*Miguel de Unamuno (1864–1936). Novelist, poet, philosopher, teacher, and rector of the University of Salamanca. Author of *Tres novelas ejemplares y un prólogo* and *Del sentimiento trágico de la vida.*

VII

℄ *On poetry. Fragments of lectures*

There is a poetry that thrives on superlatives. The poet seeks to elevate feeling by transcending time, as it were, in "uranian dimensions" of ideas. It is a poetry characteristically marked by the sensibility of the superlative—which often touches the poetical, even when the poet falls short of his intended assertion. Which means that his assertion was, at best, antipoetic. Read your Kant carefully—much less oil need be burned reading Kant than in deciphering the tenuous absurdities and Gordian tangles of dunces—and you will come upon his famous parable of the dove, who, feeling the resistance of the wind in his feathers, dreamed he would fly better in a vacuum. Thus Kant illustrates his most telling argument against dogmatic metaphysics that would also elevate itself into the absolute by an impossible flight of discursive intellect in a vacuum of intuitions. The imagery of our major philosophers, for all its dogmatic intention, has incalculable value for poetry, and some day we shall turn to it in detail. For the moment, it is enough to point out that a lyrical dove who, I firmly believe, would abrogate temporality the better to launch itself into the eternal does exist, and that, like the dove of Kant, he is unaware of the laws of its flight.

℄ Yet, would our poets sing at all without the anguish of temporality, without the sad disposition that things are never with us as they are with God: intact and at one with each other, but disposed in a series—packed into clips like rifle bullets, as it were, to be discharged one after another? That we must wait until the egg fries or the door opens or the cucumber ripens is something that merits your reflection, gentlemen. To the extent that our lives coincide with our consciousness, time is the ultimate reality, hostile to the exhortations of logic, irreducible, inviolable, fatal. To live is to devour time—to wait—and however transcendent our vigil, it will always be a vigil in which we go on waiting. Even the beatific life, that guerdon of the righteous, could it really, if it is to be a life, unfold beyond time and beyond waiting? I withhold the word "hope" designedly, which is one of those grandiose superlatives that denote our expectation of transcendent rewards, beyond which there would be nothing to wait for. As a word, it embraces theological assumptions out of place in a class in rhetoric and poetics. And I happily omit all talk of hell, to spare your fantasies a disagreeable jolt. Suffice it to say that there in the abyss one abandons all hope, in the theological sense, but not all time or the expectation of an infinite series of calamities. Hell is the bloodcurdling mansion of time, in whose profoundest circle Satan himself waits, winding a gargantuan watch in his hand.

¶ I have had occasion to define poetry as man's dialogue with time, and to call certain poets "pure" because they empty themselves of their personal time, in order to grapple alone, or almost alone, with time as such; rather as though one would chat with the buzzing in one's own ears, that most basic sonal manifestation of temporal flux. We agreed, in short, that poetry is the word in its time, and that the task of the teacher of poetics is to teach his students to maximize the temporality of their verse. All our class exercises—what could be more practical than a class in poetics—have been devoted to this end, even our most elementary ventures, one of which I remember: a poem called "Boiling the Egg," a piece written in octaves, that did not please everybody, but was by no means utterly worthless. We found, in effect, some serviceable images for lyrically transcribing basic culinary procedure—the little alcohol burner flaming bluely, the metal utensil, the agitation of the water, the little hourglass for timing—and we even ventured some others to suggest our engrossment and impatience. What was lacking was the central intuition from which the poem should have started in the first place; our solicitude for the egg never entered into the matter at all; we forgot the egg because we never truly saw it, were unable to live inside the whole process of its cooking and make it our own.

VIII

Fragments of lectures

A better definition of poetry than this never existed: "Poetry is something which poets make." However, never inquire too curiously into the "something." No poet will ever enlighten you.

And if you direct your question to teachers of literature? We will answer you, of course, because that is what we are here for: it is our pedagogical obligation. "Poetry, gentlemen, is the residue left after a delicate critical operation, which consists in eliminating from all that passes for poetry all that is not. It is a hard feat to accomplish. Because, to remove from what passes for poetry the antipoetic dross and detritus that clings to it, we would have to know what poetry is not; and to know that, in turn, we would have to know what it is. If we knew that to begin with, the whole process would be superfluous though diverting; the truth is we do not know, and the process is quite beyond realization."

And suppose you went on to the philosophers? They would tell you that your question was utterly ingenuous and that, in the last analysis, they felt under no obligation to answer you. It has never been the practice of philosophers to ask what poetry is but what is the thing that a thing really is, and whether it is possible to know something about anything, or whether we must content ourselves with never knowing anything about anything that merits our knowing.

We must talk shyly about poetry, without presuming to define it, much less deduce it by a "pure chemistry" of experimental procedure.

IX

☾ *"Don Nadie (Nobody) at Court"—sketch for a comedy in three acts by Juan de Mairena*

ACT ONE

ONLY SCENE

A Gentleman of Station, Claudio (his servant)

G. O. S.: Tell me, Claudio, did anybody call here this morning?
C.: Somebody who asked for you.
G. O. S.: Well, who was it?
C.: Somebody.
G. O. S.: Didn't he leave his name?
C.: You see what a memory I have! He gave me this card.
G. O. S. (*reading*): 'José María Nobody, Shopkeeper.' (To Claudio) If he comes back, show him in.

CURTAIN

ACT TWO

ONLY SCENE

Gentleman of Station, Claudio

G. O. S.: Has Don José María Nobody shown up?
C.: Not that I know of.
G. O. S.: Did nobody else ask for me?
C.: Nobody.
G. O. S.: Nobody?
C.: Nobody.

CURTAIN

THIRD ACT

ONLY SCENE

☾ *Gentleman of Station, Claudio, A boudoir looking glass (to function as dialogue indicates)*

G. O. S.: Tell me, Claudio, what's got into this mirror?

C.: Got into it?

G. O. S.: Whenever I try to look at myself in this mirror, it turns over like a bell—see!—and shows me the wooden side.

C.: It does at that! Upon my word!

G. O. S.: Afterward—you see!—it goes back to its normal position, with nobody even touching it. Try it for yourself.

C.: H-m-m-m! It doesn't budge for me when I look in it, sir. Try it yourself now.

G. O. S.: There now! There it goes again! (*Furious*) Well, I'll be damned!

C.: Upon my word, that's odd!

G. O. S.: Damn it all! (*Hoarsely*) Claudio, tell me, who came here this morning?

C.: This morning Don José María Nobody came to call. He got tired of waiting for you, and he left. He said he wouldn't be back.

CURTAIN

ℭ *On poetical time*

Poetry, Mairena maintained, is the dialogue of mankind: of a man with his own time. The poet would eternize it if he could, disengaging it wholly from time—a difficult and time-consuming labor requiring almost all the time given a poet to accomplish. The poet is a fisher in time: not of fish in the sea, but the whole living catch; let us be clear about that: of the fish who go on living in the aftermath of the catch.

X

☾ Echegaray,* in his tragic legend *Bosom of This Death* exclaims, in the person of the Conde de Argelez: "I, to avenge myself and torment you the more take the whole eternity of time for my own."

As if to say: "I will reckon with the Great Carp himself, to avenge myself on all fishes." Nevertheless, Echegaray, a poet-engineer of some poetical ingenuity, is not so much opposing the concept of eternity to time as postulating an eternity in time —viable time, that is to say, unendingly measured by the consciousness. This is eternity as the man in the street views it, a concept basically more tragic than the metaphysician's. What Echegaray is saying really comes to this: "I will reckon with the sea itself, to castigate all fishes."

☾ "Today we take up Lesson 28, gentlemen: our first devoted entirely to sacred oratory. Today let us chat about God. Does the theme please?"

Signs of approbation from the class.

"All those believing in God, get up on your feet."

The entire class rises, though not with equal alacrity.

"Bravo! That will do beautifully. Dismissed, gentlemen."

"? ? ? ?"

"I said you may leave."

"And what do we take up tomorrow?"

"Lesson 29: On the possible nonexistence of God."

---

*José de Echegaray (1832–1916). Author of some seventy-four melodramas, comedies, and minor pieces in prose and verse treating of "woe, lamentation, and death" in romantic style.

XI

ℭ *On Don Juan*

Don Juan is the lady's man par excellence, the man beloved and disputed by women, whom men will always regard with a certain envious disdain or a certain disdainful envy. We must take for granted, in his case, that beauty of person which women deem appropriate to the gallant. That is to say, the sexual reflection of Don Juan, his image as seen in the feminine mirror, must always be virile. Don Juan may be handsome or ill-featured, feeble or strong, one-eyed or sound as a bell: he knows, in any case, that he will dazzle the ladies. Without this conviction, Donjuanism is impossible.

Is there something perverse in Don Juan, perhaps? His detractors would like to see something feminine in this type of lady-killer. Erotic envy finds a certain comfort in demonstrating as far as it can—especially to women—that Don Juan, the well-favored Don Juan, was nothing more than an invert. The paradox, always an alluring one, is utterly untenable. The least innuendo of sexual deviation destroys the essence of the Donjuanesque: his constant orientation toward woman. Some of his feminine detractors accuse him of narcissism. Women, always derogated by Don Juan, contend that he loved nobody but himself, was actually enamored of his own image, like Narcissus. But that is an illusion of feminine jealousy, the projection of a cult of Donjuanism concocted by women. No. Don Juan, hurriedly helped into his clothing by servants, wasted no time upon mirrors. To shipwreck in a mirror, like the son of Leiriope—what arrant folly!

Don Juan appears at the dawn of the Renaissance, in a social order still marked by Church hierarchy, in a satanic and blasphemous guise. Not an atom of paganism, much less of Hebraism, of the Old Testament, is present in his make-up. Don Juan is the hero of the Christian temper. His rape of a nun, with no thought of begetting her children, is typical. In a lull in the procreative Eros, Don Juan never renounces the flesh but, like a proper monk, only the possibility of begetting in the flesh. When

Don Juan repents, he turns into a friar—which he always was, in a sense; rarely a paterfamilias.

And at what point, my teacher used to ask, does Don Juan, the supernumerary male, with no mind to the increase of Adam's line, remove himself from his species? Does he swell the Malthusian tide any more than an onanist or a homosexual? Many men, notably family men weary of the fecundity of their marital bed, are especially partial to this view. Is Don Juan, on the contrary, an aphrodisiacal mutation who speaks to the fantasies of women, to combat their habitual and natural frigidity? Who is to say? Such questions have no bearing on the essence of Don Juan but on his utility. They do not merit our interest.

℄ Avoid literary preciosity, that archenemy of originality. Bear in mind that the language you are using is already fully matured, replete with folklore and popular wisdom, and that out of this blessed clay Cervantes conjured the most original literary creation of all time. Never forget, on the other hand, that even preciosity, lost in frivolous novelty, pure incrustation, is preferable to work which shirks the basic obligations of the writer: to work into the stuff of his art the double stamp of his heart and his mind. Your defeat will be all the greater if you plunge into puristic excesses, in the belief that the repudiation of all influences from abroad is a kind of cultural accomplishment.

℄ *Mairena fantasizes*

Imagine a world in which the stones are free to elect the manner of their falling and men can do nothing at all to deflect their trajectory, forced to revolve on a circular track. That would be the infernal zone to which Dante would have committed all determinists.

Politically speaking, however, we have no problem. In such a world all men would be liberals, and the stones would go on being conservatives.

XII

ℭ *On Democritus and his atoms*

According to Democritus, the "sweet" and the "bitter," the "hot" and the "cold," the "yellow" and the "green," and so on, are nothing but opinions; only the atoms and the void are verities. For Democritus, opinion was cloudy perception, without the least guarantee of reality. Of course, gentlemen, all this is nothing but an opinion of Democritus' which no one is obliged to accept. Nevertheless, science, in the course of centuries, has been shaping a purely mechanistic concept of the universe in the spirit of Democritus' opinion—a concept which, *mutatis mutandis,* has been passed on to us, poor devils digging away at our physics, after some decades of delay, in the twilight of the nineteenth century. We cannot easily laugh off Democritus without betraying an even greater ignorance than is ours already—which is in essence considerable. I put it to you: if we accept the opinion of Democritus and all it implies, what are we: poor poet-apprentices, enamored of the sweet and the bitter, the hot and the cold, the green and the blue, and all the rest of it—not excluding good and evil—all of which bear no resemblance whatsoever to atoms or the void in which they move? Would we not be the vacuum within the void itself, lacking even the mobility of atoms? Consider the tragedy of such a predicament. For even if we could salvage some semblance of being, a reality more or less open to dispute, there would always be the fact that the atoms can exist without us, but we can never attain to being, without the atoms. And that for us is a more tragic rebuff than any plunge into absolute nothingness.

Apparently, we must choose a position, as the philosophers have it: a defensive position, let me add, arching our backs and baring our claws like a cat before the ancient concept of the mastermind from Thrace. Skepticism will come to our rescue—a skepticism which, far from being, as many like to think, a mere compulsion to deny everything, is often the only means of defending our interests. First, let us begin by doubting the existence of atoms. Then let us accept them, with certain reservations. Granting even the certainty that our existence is impossible without atoms, and that it is all a matter of atoms in the end—surely, it is equally as certain that the atoms cannot exist without us, and must manifest themselves to our consciousness in the end: that our consciousness encompasses them just as it does the colors of the rainbow and the painted plumage of the peacock's feather. What metaphysical point can there be, my teacher used to ask, in a postulate of greater or lesser reality, however faded or vividly it shows itself to our consciousness, so long as, just beyond consciousness, reality and unreality are equally undemonstrable? Only when philosophers understand this clearly and construe it for us plainly can we achieve that metaphysics for the poet which my teacher always dreamed of and for which there is such palpable need.

And now, to our lasts, gentlemen! Sing the great Democritus of Abdera, not only for the agreeable sound of his name, but above all because we have come to see, or to imagine, after twenty-four centuries—approximately (Mairena was never sure of his arithmetic)—that shadowy frown of a thinker in the magnificent act of *dis-imagining* the universal egg, sucking it dry, the white and the yolk of it, till all is vacancy, and filling it again with imperceptible particles in more or less violent motion, and bearing this prize to the mathematical sciences of the future. Here is the crowning act of the negative *poiesis* of Democritus, demolishing and creative—in the special sense my teacher gave to the word—at once. It is ours to take up that song, leaving a place in our poem for those jovial humors—who would have guessed it?—that legend has always accorded him: the nobility of his life and the easy serenity of his dying.

¶ Mairena's notion of folklore differed from that of our contemporary folklorists. For him, folklore was not a reminiscent study of ancient cultures or atavistic traits unconsciously evoked by the soul of a people in its language, practices, customs, and so on. Mairena lived in a large Andalusian township comprised of a somewhat Boeotian bourgeoisie, a highly agrarian aristocracy, and a community of alert, sensitive, and estimable craftsmen who knew their trades and were more concerned with making things well than with turning things out. Whenever someone deplored the scant facilities and parsimonious atmosphere of the university, Mairena, who had spent his student years there and regarded it with affection and esteem, always replied: "I'm afraid the reasons are much deeper than you think. Speaking confidentially, it is very possible that the erudition of our academies can never compete with our folklore, with the native insights of our people. The people are better informed and wiser than we are. A man who knows how to make something perfect in its own way—a shoe, a hat, a brick, a guitar—is more than an ingenuous drudge who hews to the line of stereotypes and formulas; he is an artist who puts all his soul into his work, every moment he is working. It is hard to hoodwink such a man with half-knowledge or counterfeit procedures." For Mairena, folklore was the viable and creative culture of a people from whom he had much to learn if he was to improve his teaching of the privileged classes.

℄ El Greco is the explosion of Michelangelo. All that is most dynamic in the baroque style begins in Buonarroti and ends in Domenico Teotocopulo. If the baroque produced anything else of comparable dynamism, it would be in the theater. Calderón is a perfect example.

℄ In every moral catastrophe, only the cynical virtues emerge unscathed. Doggy virtues, perhaps? Of the human bulldog, loyal to itself.

℄ The "new sensibility" is an expression that I have often come upon in the writings of others and have employed myself on occasion. I must confess I am not really sure what it means. A new sensibility would be hard to observe in biological terms, and might well be imperceptible during the lifetime of a zoölogical species. "New modes of feeling" sounds even worse, but is by no means inept. Feelings change in the course of history, and even in the lifetime of an individual. However agreeably they may resonate against existing notions of value, feelings will alter as values tarnish a little, or grow moldy, or give way to other values. Certain sentiments persist through the centuries, though there is no need to talk of eternal sentiments. Through how many eons has the feeling of fatherland survived? Or the paternal sentiment? And within the ambience of the sentiment itself, what a wide range of textures and degrees of feeling is contained! There are those who sob at the passing of a flag; others who respectfully uncover; others who watch the parade with indifference; others who follow the colors with hate and aversion. There is nothing as ephemeral as a feeling. Poets who believe it is enough to feel deeply to touch the eternal had better learn that.

¶ There are writers whose words seem to launch out in quest of ideas; others whose ideas seem to wait for the words which interpret them. There are even unclassifiable writers—by no means the worst—who improvise by reflection and correct by inspiration.

¶ Don't labor to correct everything. Stand up for the merits of your defects a little. There are defects that are oversights, negligences, peccadillos, matters requiring correction and soon righted; there are others which mark genuine limitations, impasses, and dead ends that vanity impels us to cover up. And that is far worse than flaunting our failings before the world.

XIII

℄ In the vanguard of skeptical pragmatism there is always a sect of idealists who, challenging skeptical pragmatism for pragmatic reasons, announce a Platonic revival, when in reality they are merely camouflaging Protagoras. It is common procedure in our times to live in a welter of contradictions without giving the matter much thought—or, worse still, hypocritically concealing the truth. Nothing is more mischievous than an unconscious skepticism, or an unacknowledged sophism, which pretends to erect a positive philosophy on a metaphysical negation that is really an agnostic's faith. Bah! When man ceases to believe in the absolute, he believes nothing at all. For all belief is belief in the absolute. The rest is mere thinking.

℄ The Spaniard, as often as not, is a decent soul, generally inclined to piety. Wanton cruelty—in spite of our *afición* for the bulls—has never been highly esteemed in Spain. On the other hand, we are notably lacking in respect, fellow feeling, and—above all—gratification at the successes of others. If you see a bullfighter execute a flawless series of passes in the ring, while the whole plaza batters its palms in wild pandemonium—wait a moment. When all has simmered down again you will invariably see a man heaving up to his feet, thrusting two fingers into his mouth, and caterwauling with all the strength of his lungs. Don't imagine he is hissing the bullfighter; he was probably applauding with the others—his catcalls are for the applause.

℄ I would urge you to be a little better than you really are but never to be less than a Spaniard. No one is more committed to the virtues of our race or fonder of them than I am. Among these I include the ability to judge ourselves severely and view our neighbors with indulgence. We must be utterly Spanish, to say what needs to be said against ourselves. In doing so, we need fear nothing that smacks of the unnatural or the inexplicable.

For no one can shed light on vices he does not have or afflictions he has never experienced. It is an honorable condition, profoundly and sincerely human. I suggest that you persevere in it all your lives.

Those who regard Spain as a kind of trademark, to be defended and accredited at all costs in the world market, for whom both the publicity and approval of our vices and the cloaking of them are equally a patriotic duty, may merit, I grant you, the epithet of good patriots—but never of good Spaniards.

I call them good patriots only because they look upon Spain, like all the other nations of Europe, as an essentially embattled entity fated to join in a massive contention; to which end they seek to minimize all vacillation and maximize our polemical force, including our national pride, however synthetically induced. But such thinking is profoundly un-Spanish. Spain has never battled for national pride or pride of race as such, but for pride in the human condition or love of God—which comes to the same thing.

XIV

❨ *From a discourse by Juan de Mairena*

Only in moments of sloth does a poet address himself to the interpretation of his dreams and rummage there for odds and ends useful to him as a poet. Oneiromancy has never yet produced anything of consequence. The poems written in our wakefulness, even the less finished, are lovelier and more original—and at times more chimerical—than anything encountered in dreams. Take the word of one who has spent years believing otherwise: change is the beginning of wisdom.

To see things as they are, the eyes must be open; to see things as other than they are, they must open even wider; to see things as better than they are, they must be open to the full. Vigilance is all, if your purpose is to see and imagine the world wakefully and if you are not to ask in its place for the uneasy repose of the dreamer.

❨

> All that fine
> frenzy of nightingales singing! . . .
> Not a word of it is mine.

So sang the poet for whom the world was beginning to take on a new magic. "The charm of the nightingales," he would tell us, "lies in the fact that they sing of their own loves and never of ours." The observation is much more than a truism: it encompasses a whole metaphysic that is, in its own way, a whole new system of poetics. New? As new as anything in this old world, to be sure. For the world is innately pristine: whatever the poet invents or discovers with each passing moment—though this does not always include new self-knowledge, as many would like to think—is always something new under the sun. To achieve the creative, poetic reflection must grasp the essential and irreducible differences, and not the equations, of things; for only by touching the Other, either actual or apparent, can the outcome be fruitful. I therefore oppose to logical and mathematical reflection—with its essentially homogenizing drive, dedicated, in the last analysis, to the contemplation of Nothingness—the necessary heterogeneity of poetic thought. Forgive the jargon of vested erudition; this is a classroom, after all, and every rostrum has its passing pedant.

XV

☾ It has been observed, on occasion, that the poet is he who sees further into the future, "into the seeds of time," as Shakespeare has it. This is generally said with Goethe in mind, whose prognosis of the human and divine state has long overpowered us by its truth. But Goethe is not the only poet in the world; there are greater than Goethe, who have been, above all other things, clairvoyants of the *past.* Assuredly, seeing is of the essence of poetry and, like all vision, requires distance; we must pardon the poet, therefore, rapt on the coming and going of things, if he rarely has eyes for the immediate datum—the images that batter his eyes and which we would all gather, if we could, in handfuls.

What we call actuality is the wind in the eyes of Homer, the many-sounding sea in his ears.

☾ *Two great inventions*

The Platonic faith in transcendent ideas saved the Greek world from the *solus ipse* in which its sophists would have enveloped it. Human reason is generic thinking. Whoever reasons affirms the existence of his neighbor, the necessity for dialogue, the possibility of intellectual communion between all men. It is important to believe in Platonic ideas without denigrating the traditional view of Platonism. Without the absolute transcendency of ideas—alike for all, intuitable and incorruptible to individual thought—reason, as the common matrix for plurality of spirit, could neither exist nor have a reason for being. We must leave the interpretation of "true" Platonic thought to the philosophers. For us, essential Platonism is a faith in the metaphysical reality of ideas that passing centuries have never destroyed.

☾ Platonism, Mairena continued, was a triumphant attainment, but not enough to banish man's solitude. Whoever converses, to be sure, affirms the reality of his neighbor—the "I" that is not his own; all the apparatus of reasoning—truths and assumptions alike—imply a modus vivendi on the part of the reasoning partners, or the common vision of an ideal object. But reason—that Socratic invention—is not enough to insure human community; heartfelt communion, the convergence of feelings on a common object of love, is also important. This was the accomplishment of Christ: a Promethean feat and, in a certain sense, a satanic one. For my teacher, Abel Martín, Christ was a wayward angel, a youth rebelling against the regimen of the Father. Put it another way: Christ was the man who made Himself God to expiate on the Cross the cardinal sin of divinity. From this point of view, my teacher reasoned, the tragedy of Golgotha acquires new significance and another dimension of grandeur.

Christ, in effect, rebels against the law of Israel's God, the God of a people committed to a mission of survival in time. The God of Israel embodies that divinized procreative virtue whose law aims solely at the propagation and conservation of the seed. In the name of this "proletarian" ("proles"="offspring") God, Christ was crucified—son of nobody at all, in the Jewish sense: an incarnation of divine spirit with no carnal mission to accomplish. Who was this offspring of nobody, whose message is love and who makes no effort to beget love in the flesh? All that heritage of blood kinship, all that spending of semen, to arrive at—*this*! Thus, the sons of Israel directed their proletarian wrath at the Son of God, brother of mankind. And thus Christ's word challenged the patriarchal sense of their history.

If we eliminate from the Evangels their Mosaic incrustations, the teaching of Christ is clear enough: "There is only one Father, the Father of us all, Who is in Heaven." Here is the transcendent erotic object, the fervent idea on which a structure of human fraternity was reared for the ages. Filial obligations? There was only one: infinite love for the Father of all, whose impress, more or less faded, we all bear in our souls. The rest is a rubric of brotherly virtues and duties. Christ, by the mere fact of having been born, superseded for all time the procreative obsession of Biblical Judaism. Just as Socrates triumphed over the Protagorean sophistry of his day, lighting the way to the idea, to the necessary intellectual communion of men, Christ triumphed over the erotic sophistry that burdened the spirit of the pagan world, revealing a new destiny for humanity: that of love. These are the two great masters of dialectic, who knew how to question and wait for the answers. They are neither charlatans nor pedants. Charlatans and pedants are only chatterers who listen to no one, least of all themselves. The dialectic of Christ is, however, quite foreign to that of Socrates: more subtle and luminous. We will get to that another time, when we take up another theme: "Woman as the invention of Christ." *Fragment of a discourse by Juan de Mairena, known to his pupils as the "Sermon at Chipiona."*

XVI

¶ *Memoirs and memoranda of Juan de Mairena*

Our century (Juan de Mairena meant, of course, the nineteenth) is perhaps the most self-engrossed of centuries, because, it may be, those of us who lived in it have a morbidly temporal sense of our existence. The man of our century has been a self-styled *enfant du siècle*, given to talk of a *mal du siècle*, and is lately preoccupied with a *fin de siècle*. In this way he expresses, more or less consciously, a penchant for temporality by no means typical of all ages.

We have exalted, *ad nauseam*, music and lyric poetry, surely the most temporal of the arts. Our architecture and sculpture are meager. Our painting has been naturalist, impressionist, luminist—all temporal modes of the graphic. History, which spoke of timeless and mythical man to a classical world, has plunged headlong into time and emptied the epic into the novel and the newspaper—in effect, pulverized the timeless and shredded it into topical anecdotes and events of the week. Our drama is neither art, nor logic, nor ethics, but psychologistic, which is a temporal mode of theatrical dialogue. Our typical philosophy is positivism, contemporanized thinking, which has triumphed, so say its exemplars, over one age of metaphysics and another of theology. In politics, we have battled for progress and tradition, two temporal illusions. Our sciences are biologistic and evolutionary, a mystique of vital fact amenable to temporal law. Lamartine weeps with the romantics—who of this great century is not a romantic?—at the *fugit irreparabile tempus*, while Carnot and Clausius, in their thermodynamics, deliver the basic law of nature over to time.

Such is our century, gentlemen—your fathers' century, basically—but still yours, however you press past its frontiers. An interesting century of sorts, for those who would fathom man's sojourn in the world—neither greater nor lesser, wiser nor stupider, than others which have left their mark on our culture—but perhaps the century of all centuries the most *lapsed* in its time and the most century-minded, because none was more constant in its self-obsession.

◖ Juan de Mairena, who died in the first years of the twentieth century, preserved to the end his nineteenth-century faith in the belief that centuries do not begin and conclude with the chronological exactitude one might wish, and that certain centuries, like his own, might well go on for a century and a half. Mairena never lived to see the First World War, and would probably have called it the crash of the century; or the triumph and vogue of Henri Bergson; or that most fascinating of all posthumous nineteenth-century documents, Proust's *À la recherche du temps perdu*, where we see, for the last time perhaps, the faded and fraying *enfant du siècle*, no longer the well-shod young bourgeois, stripped of his Napoleonic euphoria and all the romantic pathos lavished on him by Balzac and Stendhal, Lamartine and Musset. "*Voilà enfin,*" Mairena often said, "*un vrai fin de siècle!*" It was in Proust's little mannikin—him above all!—that Mairena would have come to sense the concluding modulations and initiating motifs of his century's melody. For what Proust gives us in effect is a romantic poem in the manner of a decadent novel, a poem of youth evoked from old age. *Le temps perdu* is truly the artist's century seen as time past which can never attain to time future, and in which all that is not remembered is irretrievably lost.

XVII

℄ Skepticism may or may not be fashionable. I do not suggest that you swell the ranks of either its proponents or its detractors. I suggest rather that you take a skeptical stance in relation to skepticism. For example, when I think that truth does not exist, I will also think that it might, precisely for having thought the contrary; for as there is no valid reason for believing what I think is the truth, there is not too much ground for assuming truth is any less true because I think it. That way, you can have your cake and eat it too, and parry the old bromide against skeptics that is really an argument against skeptical dogmatism.

℄ *On the apocryphal*

Mairena used to tell his students: You have excellent parents who deserve your respect and affection; why not go on to invent better?

℄ *On carnival*

It is said that the festival of carnival is on its way out. What is clear, said Mairena, is that people, whenever they are moved to make merry, make carnival. In the sense that the carnivalesque is the specifically popular expression of festivity, there is little danger of its disappearance. And from a more aristocratic point of view, the threat is even less plausible. For the essence of carnival is not to put on one's mask but to put off one's face. There is no one so bound to his own face that he does not cherish the hope of presenting another to the world.

XVIII

☾ *In class*

M.: Mr. Rodríguez, do you recall what we said about concepts and intuitions?

R.: That concepts without intuitions are hollow, and that intuitions without concepts are blind. That is to say, sir, that there is no way of fleshing out concepts without intuitions, and no way of giving eyes to intuition without mustering them in a concept. Knowledge is the result of joining intuitions to concepts: the filling of a void that is at the same time blindness made clairvoyant.

M.: And you see all that clearly, of course?

R.: Clearly, dear teacher: with the cloudiest perfection.

☾ My teacher used to tell us that to think is to meander from highway to byway, and from byway into alleyway, till we come to a dead end. Stopped dead in our alley, we think what a feat it would be to get out. That is when we look for the gate to the meadows beyond.

XIX

ℭ *Frivolous prophecies of Juan de Mairena*

Juan de Mairena used to say: Where woman is customarily "kept in her place," as in Spain, where she is a homebody, wedded to the hearth and the rearing of children, she usually dominates and stamps her will on the total fabric of a society. The real problem in that case is the emancipation of the male from the inflexible regimen of the matriarch. Where women go voteless in public life, they call the tune and cast the decisive ballot in all other matters. Even if certain suffragist viragoes who abound the world over should exact from male frivolity the right to vote in Spain, the rank and file of womanhood would vote down the franchise; that is to say, they would bury under their ballots any political regime imprudent enough to grant them an option they never desired. That would be the first move. If it later so happened that women sought to intervene in public life and demanded their franchise, knowing perfectly well what that involved, rest assured that the initiative of the Spanish matriarchate is beginning to ebb and that the men are setting the pace for the women, rather than the other way round. The occasion would then be profoundly revolutionary. But the peril is so remote we need not ponder it unduly.

ℭ *Mairena as playwright*

"What a loving father is now lost to the world!" So cries Jack the Ripper a few moments before he is strangled by the hangman's noose in Mairena's tragic play *Father and Fiend,* whistled off the boards in a hubbub in Seville in the last years of the century.

Mairena's Jack was a man much given to loving—more than seventy women, all told, counting the wives and the camp followers—in the firm expectation, always unrealized, of begetting a child. The sterility of his connubial bed first drove him to melancholy, then to desperation, and finally to hatred, insanity, and unnatural crime. The play was performed to timid applause and murmurs of disapproval. Some held it to be "Not bad, really"; others found it "Daring"; others, "Insupportable!" After the curtain line: "What a loving father is now lost to the world!" uttered with deep feeling by Don Pedro Delgado, one of Mairena's students shouted in stentorian tones: "Bravo, maestro!" That was when bedlam broke loose. Mairena never wrote for the theater again, fearing another debacle from an audience insufficiently prepared for the tragic. That same season, however, a *Nero* by Cavestany made its debut, with highly complimentary notices.

℄ Men of repute should beware of the dimming of their legend—every celebrity lives with one, from the time of his major successes—even though legend is the child of our inveterate misunderstanding of our neighbor. A lifetime is not time enough to tear down one legend and erect another. And lacking a legend, no one passes on into history.

XX

℄ Of the dramatic pieces written by Juan de Mairena, without any thought to their presentation, one, a tragicomedy entitled *The Grand Climacteric* remains memorable. The protagonist, always on stage, is a personage symbolizing the "unconscious libido" in human existence, from adolescence to the culmination of sexual effectiveness, a date which physicians used to fix at sixty-three for males—and which Mairena, treading thin ice, assigned to both sexes.

In all the twenty-one acts of this work there is not the slightest anticipation of Freud or other celebrated psychiatrists of our day; but there are a number of interesting innovations—none of them startling—in theatrical techniques. The dialogue, for one thing, is accompanied by musical "illustrations." Guitars and cornets take the role of commentators, joyous and bantering at some times, and lashing up catastrophe by subtle and minimal stages, like a classical chorus, at others. Mairena sought to restore to drama—this was the most original aspect of his technique—the monologues and asides long since abandoned by playwrights, and give new scope to their function. He did so for a number of reasons, which he explained in class to his students.

1. By this means, Mairena maintained, some of the innocence lost to the theater and much of its earlier probity would be restored. A comedy of monologues and asides is straightforward playmaking: all the cards are on the table, as in Shakespeare, in Lope, in Calderón. We have nothing to probe for except spiritual blind spots; on all other matters the actor will constantly enlighten us, either in open dialogue, or in soliloquies, interior monologues, asides, and the mental hesitations that might well lie just on the other side of our conversation.

2. The canned comedy and drama of facile psychologism whose progressions thrive on the arbitrary concealment of trivial conscious developments, forcing us to infer the facts from a drivel of dialogue, inhibitions, fragmentary phrases, pauses,

gestures, and so on, so difficult to grasp on a stage, would disappear from the theater.

3. The theater would be delivered from the "confidant," that superfluous and passive catchall, untouched by the action of the play, whose single mission it is to draw out—for the benefit of the audience—whatever the operative protagonists can never say to each other, but which each would readily admit to himself and tell us in monologues and asides.

(One of Mairena's pupils offered the following observation to his teacher:

"The theater of today, predominantly realistic, makes a point of avoiding the conventional and implausible. Is it so very plausible that anyone would talk to himself in full hearing of a friend, or even when he is alone, except in moments of exaltation or insanity?"

"Capital!" Mairena exclaimed, favoring his pupil's tact with a good-humored chortle. "But have *you* reckoned with the fact that the curtain of a modern theater almost always rises and falls on a room with three walls, in which the fourth wall we all count on is missing? Why not ponder that glaring improbability as well?"

"But how are we to know what is taking place in the room with a fourth wall in front of us?" the student answered Mairena.

"And how are we to know what is taking place inside a character, if he does not step forth and divulge it?"

(Mairena went on to observe: Before venturing into non-Euclidian, four-dimensional comedy—I put it this way to capture the attention of the advance guard—we shall have to restore and refurbish the much-maligned cubical comedy of three dimensions that has all but disappeared from the scene. Think of it, friends: in the theater which you are calling modern and realistic and which I would call psychologistic and didactic, the genre most committed to drama-in-depth has been relentlessly and persistently flattening itself out. Here, as in so many other things, our era abounds in contradictions.

℄ Because it is natural to live more or less intimately with oneself, and in only occasional proximity with others, the people in my comedy (Mairena had in mind his *Grand Climacteric*) cannot function as mere conversationalists, self-propelled silences, empty and impenetrable solitudes. Like the characters of Shakespeare, whose actions are accompanied by changing intensities of consciousness, they must be men and women whose conversation is often less salient than their monologues and asides. Recall Hamlet, Macbeth, and other imperishable titans of that artist in consciousness—what greater feat can poets aspire to? When they arrive at self-knowledge they not only tell us all about themselves but press us to go further and infer whatever it is that eluded them.

℄ The musical part of my work *The Grand Climacteric* has been reduced to a handful of notes. And even these may be dispensed with if the comedy is ever (posthumously!) presented. However, you are not to assume that the music was introduced without good esthetic and psychological reason. If our theater is to be fully expressive, it must provide for the voice of the subconscious, since it is there, I believe, that the most volatile and intimate sources of action originate. Let us bypass that issue for the moment and sum up.

We have, as essential elements of "cubical" theater, the following:

1. What the characters say to each other, tête-à-tête—dialogue in the most direct sense of the word, as it is used and abused in contemporary drama. This is the outermost layer of comedy, where dialogue in the Socratic sense of the term is never even contemplated: a colloquium in which everyone competes with a trivial ideology of his own. For example:

"Why should a lady of my breeding ever have to lose her heart to a Sergeant of the Revenue Guard?"

"What do you think, Duchess?"

"Oh, nothing really. But you know very well, my dear Marquis, there's no limit to slander."

"I blush to confess it; who hasn't dabbled in slander sometime or other?"

"Well, I should never be one to cast the first stone."
"Or I the second, if it comes to that."
"Always the well-spoken gallant . . ."

Actors excel in this kind of dialogue; they are past masters in the art of reducing everything to unimportance.

2. The monologues and asides that disclose latent feelings and motivations and reveal, for example, that the soul of Macbeth is a ferment of kingly ambition, a determination to murder Duncan, and even the fatal action itself, as it ripens in the terrible soliloquy:

> Is this a dagger which I see before me,
> The handle towards my hand?

Or take the example cited above, our little scene between the Duchess and the Sergeant of the Revenue Guard—or rather, her harrowing memory of the Sergeant—surely we would want a monologue in which she commends herself to God's mercy, exhorts Him to preserve her womanly pride and blameless good name as a spouse and to deliver her from evil temptations.

To communicate all this we must, of course, have actors capable of feeling, understanding, and, above all, imagining dramatic identities in crises and predicaments that are no mere copies of ordinary life.

3. Apprised by the dialogue, the monologues, and asides of all the protagonist has come to grasp of his predicament, the total content of his conscious self-knowledge, we can proceed with the "oblique tactics" of comedy to suggest all that evades open disclosure: profound and primordial things, unconscious and subconscious depths out of which well the seminal forces of conscience and action: the cosmic vitality that, in the last analysis, dynamizes all drama—the *Olé*! *Olé*! of things, compelling and baffling at once, that will hurl our poor heroine inevitably into the arms of the Sergeant of the Guard.

For this purpose only, I require the assistance of musical rubrics. Convinced as I am, however, that the mixing of media breeds nothing but hybrids, esthetically sterile in themselves, I have almost decided to dispense with such pentagrams altogether.

XXI

℄ *On theater*

Mairena remarked to his students: Why did I call my tragicomedy *The Grand Climacteric*? For one thing, the sound of it pleased me: it seemed right for a tragical drama that might also turn into a comedy of humors, or vice versa. For another thing, as I have already pointed out, it focuses attention on the sixty-third year of our lives, which physicians and astrologists agree is the most crucial and hazardous—the *klimakter,* or "step of the stair," the most difficult to surmount, after which we all lapse into old age, surrender our sexual force, and come to the end of our erotic tragicomedy: with some valedictory reflections, no doubt, on the gamut traversed. That is the title's purpose; it makes no pretensions at summary definition.

The choice of theme—the libido or sex drive as seen through time and the mutations of man's growth—has nothing to do with a wish to blaze theatrical paths through materials that pander to morbid curiosity, lubricous allusions that gratify all that is most perverse and sinister in metropolitan taste. Not a bit of it! The theme is original—that is to say, as ancient as the world itself, and makes no bid for the approval of snobs. It has often appeared in the theater of our great century, in a number of guises. I choose it because it deeply concerns us, threshed fine by Spanish talents though it be, as an integral theme of comedy *à là española.*

℄ Remember how often I've said it: out of every ten innovations attempted, all very splendid, nine will end up in silliness; the tenth and the last, though it escape the preposterous, will show little that is new in the end. That's the way the world wags, gentlemen. It is not given man to create a world out of nothing, like a Biblical God, or to perform the miracle in reverse, like the God of my teacher: an even more difficult feat. The unprecedented, properly speaking, is forbidden us. Let us understand that plainly. Our burning desire to revitalize the theater is nothing new under the sun—nothing "novel," as our American cousins put it—but rather an effort to restore, mutatis mutandis, piecemeal and overnight, much that has been unfairly jettisoned or forgotten.

Drama belongs with the literary arts. Its mode of expression is the word. We dare not debase in our plays the high office of the word. Daily we chatter and hold forth with one another, in words; we think, feel, and desire, with words; we address ourself to our neighbors, and often to ourselves, with words; we speak to a listening God or the Devil himself, if he confronts us, with words. The great poets of the theater understood this better than we: they never limited their language to the passing inanities we employ in superfluous chatter while our minds are preoccupied with other things; they go on to utter that other thing on which interest universally centers.

¶ The dramatic, Mairena continued, as I will never tire of repeating, demands action: specifically, human action accompanied by the phenomenon of consciousness—of words, among other things. Where the function of language deteriorates, there will follow a like impoverishment of action. Only those who confuse action with gesticulation, the bustle of entrances and exits, can have failed to observe that dramatic action—forgive the redundancy—has been gradually disappearing from the theater. The evil is plain to others—above all, the general public, who no longer come to see comedies played but keep to their houses. Lacking words, and with them, the action requisite to drama, could our theater without the aid of spectacle hope to compete with a day at the circus or an amateur bullfight in the provinces? Only a wave of puerile extravagance, more or less kinesthetic, billowing up from America will ever compensate us for the dramatic inconsequence that is left us. But that is not resurrecting the theater; it is more like a premature wake.

XXII

℄ Mairena used to say to his students: Before writing a poem, one must imagine a poet capable of writing it. The poem once written, we can preserve both the poet and his poem; or disengage the poet and publish his poem, which is standard procedure; or toss the poem in the wastebasket and stay with the poet; or, finally, rid ourselves of both and preserve only the imagining man, keyed for new poetic experience.

These words, and certain additional remarks published in a journal at the time, did not sit well with our poets—who must have been legion, judging by the shower of stones that rained on the head of our modest professor of rhetoric.

℄ Let us assume, Mairena said, that Shakespeare, the only begetter of so many deeply human identities, went on to imagine for his own entertainment the poem each one might have written in his hours of idleness—in the entr'actes of his tragedies, as it were. Hamlet's poem would obviously be different from Macbeth's; and Romeo's would be quite other than Mercutio's. But Shakespeare would remain the author of them all, and the author of the authors of the poems.

℄ However, would you say that a man can carry no more than one poet within himself? The reverse would be much more unlikely: that he carried inside himself only one.

℄ After truth, my teacher said, there is nothing as lovely as a fiction.

The great poets are defeated metaphysicians.

The great philosophers are poets who believe in the reality of their poems.

The skepticism of poets can do much to enliven our philosophers. Similarly, poets might well learn from our philosophers the art of grandiloquent metaphor—the uses of imagery for didactic effect and the timeless intensity of poetry. Examples: "the river of Heraclitus," "the sphere of Parmenides," "the lyre of Pythagoras," "Plato's cave," and "Kant's dove."

From the philosophers the poet might also learn about blind alleys, dead ends of the mind—and escape, if he must, by the rooftops: to understand better the natural aporetic of all reason, its utter irrationality, and preserve a tolerant respect for those who proceed topsy-turvy—as Don Julian Sanz del Río used to do with his greatcoat, wearing it outside in, on the theory that that was the way to keep warmest.

¶ Juan de Mairena used to startle his students on occasion with fine phrases whose imprecision he would have been the first to acknowledge, but which, he nevertheless believed, encompassed a modicum of truth. One comes to mind, similar in style and effect—if somewhat less grandiose—to a general proposition of the great Xenius*: "In our literature," Mairena said "almost everything that isn't folklore is pedantry."

It was never Mairena's intention to belittle our literary glories with a phrase, any more than Xenius, when he announced: "All that is not traditional is plagiarism," meant to derogate tradition or surrender it to the traditionalists. By folklore, in the first place, Mairena had in mind the most literal meaning of the word: popular wisdom—the lore of the folk—as the folk themselves know it; what a people think and feel precisely as they happen to think and to feel it; the means by which they mold and express their experience in the language which they, more than anyone else, have helped to create. In the second place, he had in mind the conscious and meditative modes of manipulating these elements, the uses, both learned and creative, to which they may be put.

It is highly probable that without the old ballads and chivalric romances to serve his satirical needs, Cervantes would never

---

*Pseudonym of Eugenio D'Ors, Catalan philosopher (1883–1954), best known for his *Glosario* and *El secreto de la filosofía* (1947).

have written his *Quijote,* though he would probably have given us a work of equal genius. Without his assimilation and mastery of a language duly charged with popular wisdom and awareness, neither that immortal work nor anything faintly resembling it could ever have been composed. Of this I am certain.

Nevertheless, I fear that our teachers of Literature—I bear them no grudge, really—are inclined to mention our folklore only in passing, without going very deeply into matters or stressing the folkloric sufficiently, and to think of our literature as the outcome of exclusively learned activity. Chairs in folklore in our universities would only make matters worse: they would be appropriated by "experts"—specialists in the hunting and fishing of folkloriana, to be served in its own right, as a discipline apart. This might conceivably serve some good purpose, but is distracting and misleading, from the outset. *A Dictionary of Proverbs in Quijote,* for example, even if it were accompanied by a more or less classified study of Cervantine proverbs, would tell us little about the function of the proverb in that immortal work. I have warned you before: the fisherman knows least about fish—next to the fishmonger, who knows nothing at all. No. What Cervantists will tell us some day about folkloric aspects of *Quijote* is this, rather:

To what degree Cervantes has made them his own; how they move and embody him; how he thinks and feels with them; how he organizes and deploys them; and how often they shape his own thinking. Why the proverbial—that complex of judgment and experience, sententiousness and wit—predominates in Cervantes over simpler concepts or the concept refurbished with rhetorical artifice? How Cervantes apportions the proverbs between those two complementary souls Don Quijote and Sancho. When a whole country speaks in their persons; when the race; when mankind; and when language itself. What the perceptual worth, or the critical or the dialectical worth, of the folkloric is. Our Cervantists could tell us all this, and go on from that point.

XXIII

❨ Mairena observed to his students: When a thing is bad, my teacher often said it behooves us to imagine something good in its place; if, by chance, we have already discovered the good, we should go on to imagine something better. The movement is always from the imagined, or the supposed, or the apocryphal—never from the actual.

❨ We live in an essentially apocryphal world, a cosmos or poem of our own thinking, ordered and structured on undemonstrable suppositions postulated by reason, which we have come to call principles of logical discourse. It is these principles, compacted and synthesized into a principle of identity, that constitute the master supposition of them all: that all things, by the mere fact of their having been thought remain immutable, anchored forever, as it were, in the river of Heraclitus. The apocryphal character of our world is proved by the existence of logic—our need to put our thinking in accord with itself, to compel it in a sense to see nothing but the supposititious or its postulates, to the exclusion of all other things. In a word, the fact that our whole world is founded on a predicate which might well be erroneous is either dreadful or comforting, depending on the eye of the beholder.

❨ Now let us have a try at another possible dilemma: how inexorable the problem of the perception of the external would be if we assumed consciousness to be like a mirror that copies, reproduces, represents, and did not go on to establish that these mirrors see the images formed within them—that an image in the consciousness is equivalent to the consciousness of an image.

Even more bizarre—if not actually more preposterous—is the notion that our consciousness "translates" into its own "language" a world "written" in another; for if the other language is unknown to our consciousness, translation is hardly possible; and if the language is already known to us, what is the point of translation? For whom do we translate? No one really translates for himself, but for others unfamiliar with the language of the original—and then only if he has mastered each of the two languages. The shell game involved here—the *tour de passe-passe* that seeks to cover up our tautology—is of course our use of the verb "translate" in the context previously served by the word "represent."

More untenable still is the pragmatist's notion of consciousness as a utilitarian activity, in which we choose whatever interests us most from the life around us, and of the external world as the product of that selection. For the act of choosing presupposes a prior awareness of what is taken and what left behind. Consciousness as a sieve or strainer of the real is, of all concepts of consciousness, the most maladroit and half-baked.

Let us return, Mairena continued, to the notion of consciousness as a light moving in darkness, directing its rays on the Other—always on the Other. However, this luminous notion of consciousness—the most poetic and venerable and vested of them all—is also the most obscure, so long as we have omitted to establish that there exists a light capable of *seeing* what it illuminates. My teacher had this in mind, I believe, when, without attempting to put it to the test, he alluded to divine consciousness, or the divinizing of human consciousness in death, in imperishable verse:

> Before it be Day, if day be given indeed,
> the all-beholding light, that is not yet come to pass*

He understood that a light without vision is as blind as everything else in this world.

❨ In order to be a clown, my teacher used to say, one must first be an Englishman: one of a great nation of humorists who have grasped so profoundly the deathless epigram of the Latin co-

*See Appendix, "Death of Abel Martín," lines 25–26.

median[*]: Nothing human is alien to me—above all, the inexhaustible folly of mankind. The clown takes on himself man's folly, professes it openly like a circus buffoon, to the sober delight of children and saints. When we follow the antics of an English clown, watching and listening, the emergence of a Shakespeare, replete with antic humanity, becomes more understandable. Reading Corneille, or Racine, or even Molière, we learn nothing at all about the nature of French clowns. Reading Quevedo—let his admirers speak for themselves, if there are any. For my own part, Mairena went on, I would dare to affirm that reading Cervantes I have understood all.

¶ The lot of the satirist, that acrimonious flayer of vices and unsavory foibles, is more often than not an unhappy one because there is something bogus about it, something obtuse and provincial. It consists of utterly ignoring the fact that the vices and failings which we point to in others we have first come to see in ourselves, in disregarding the epigram cited above and in forgetting, above all, the injunction of Christ: to restrain the blithe impulse to cast the first stone at our neighbor.

¶ Epicurus says that no one need fear death because where life is, death is not, and where death is, we are not. Such a line of reasoning is presumably demolishing: it would seem we have leaped safely over the horns, like a bullfighter, with Attic presence of mind. However (Mairena's "however" always thrummed bass on the guitar of his thinking), a thrust over the horns is never so cozy as it appears, not even with the good offices of Epicurus, for at every turn of the bullfight, properly speaking, death leaps with us. This is well known to bullfighters.

¶ Even though our thoughts leap from Cadiz to Puerto, and from Puerto to Singapore, all evidence points to the fact that no one who lives in Chiclana will die in Chipiona. I, for one, am certain of that; there are not many truths of this magnitude.

---

[*]Terence (185–159 B.C.) Roman comic poet and author of six plays, including the *Eunuchus*.

Death goes with us and keeps pace with us throughout life; it is, in a word, part and parcel of our bodies. One can do worse than conceive of death as a kind of private herringbone or skeleton we carry inside us, and ponder the analogical power of the image. If we assume—and why not assume it?—the essential duality of all substance, we can never, by that right, disavow, so long as we live, our "compact" with death, as I believe Epicurus viewed it, or neglect the courtesy due to so steadfast a sojourner. Death speaks the gravest words of our language, in our own Don Jorge Manrique*:

> . . . Good sir and good knight,
> leave a pickthank
> and arduous world;
> show a soldier's renown,
> that rapier blade of your heart,
> and drink the draft down.

Before we prate of immortality—a far more rhetorical theme—we might ponder the substance of Don Jorge's exhortation: how far away it takes us from the gamey syllogisms of the cults, and the dialectical horseplay of the Epicureans.

---

*Jorge Manrique (1440–1479). Poet and soldier, whose somber and elegant *Coplas* on the death of his father are unmatched in the elegiac literature of Spain. The thirty-sixth stanza of the forty-stanza poem, here quoted, seems to have been a key passage for Machado, and is applied to the death of Abel Martín in the concluding lines of "Death of Abel Martín" (see Appendix) and to the death of Valle-Inclán (see XLI).

XXIV

❡ My teacher had a memorable maxim: There is nothing so fearful as the zeal of the priestly unbeliever. Or, putting it another way: God deliver us from apocryphal gods!—in the etymological sense of the word: occult, unconfessed, and clandestine gods. They have always been the most pitiless of all gods, and the most perverse; it is they who demand the blood sacrifice offered up to the others, the gods of the authorized cults.

❡ Outside time, that invention of Satan—outside that time which my teacher called the "spawn of Beelzebub's fall"—the world would lose both the anguish of waiting and the consolation of hope. Devils would lose their vocations; and so would the poets.

❡ To gain a great audience, it is not enough to harangue a convention. One must become a son of God, like Christ.

❡ The philosophy of history has been facetiously defined by some as the "art of prophesying the past." In point of fact, the more we reflect on the past and penetrate to its depths, the more we uncover the sum of the world's hopes, neither realized nor yet wholly unrealized: in short, that sense of futurity which has always been the legitimate content of prophecy. In any case, the art of prophesying the past is a complementary adjunct of that no less paradoxical art of turning the future into the past: which is what we do in effect whenever we relinquish a hope on the "prudent" assumption, as Don Jorge Manrique has it, that whatever might have been and is not should be consigned to the past. From another point of view, the art of prophesying the past is precisely what we have come to regard as the science—or the art—of anticipating the forseeable: that is, the already foreseen and tested, or, properly speaking, the past. Among the many gambits we live by, we cannot ever elude the need for playing at prophecy, though I would caution you always to trim your beards short and shun all usurious pretensions of infallibility.

⸿ Better no prophets at all than prophecy in the usurious manner of pawnbrokers, who peer into the future to buy possibility at less than the market price.

XXV

☾ Well, then, so we wish to be sophists in the best sense of the word or, putting it more modestly, in a benign sense of the word: we wish to be freethinkers. I see no cause for alarm. There is no reason to assume, by that right, we demand every license to heap abuse on our monarchs, or vilify governments, bishoprics, and parliaments. The free utterance of thought is a significant but secondary problem, overshadowed by a deeper concern: which is the liberty of thinking as such. The immediate problem we must put to ourselves is this: whether thought in itself, our own thinking, in the case of each one of us, has truly fulfilled its free processes, independent of all subsequent sanctions; or whether it has not. Putting it rhetorically, what good end is served by the free utterance of servile ideas? Hence the point of our classroom procedures, which seem logical to some and sophistical to others in the pejorative sense of the word; but which basically pertain to a study of rhetoric—rhetoric proper to sophists and catechumens of free thought: good rhetoric. Our aim is to strengthen and sensitize thinking, and thereby discover its real limitations and potentialities: the degree to which thinking is free, original, self-initiating, and the degree to which we are blocked by inflexible criteria, unaltering habits of mind, or the sheer impossibility of thinking differently. Beware of that chiefly; the danger lies there!

These words were transcribed by ear, by Mairena's "class listener," a student, specializing in the function of listening, whom Mairena never molested with questions. The style of his notes suggests that their author was a stenographer's apprentice, rather than a student of rhetoric. This suspicion grew on Mairena increasingly in the course of several semesters; but all that he ever said was: "A lad who really listens! My compliments to you, friend!"

XXVI

The listener

The listener in rhetoric, for whom Mairena predicted a career as congressional stenographer, was a genuine listener, the complete listener who not only scribbles away in his notebook, but listens with deepest attention at all times, frowning and smiling by turns. Mairena observed this with respect and approval, never daring to dun him outright with a question. Only once, after making the rounds of the class without satisfaction, did he single him out with a pointed forefinger, while he tried vainly to think of his name.

"You, there . . ."

"Joaquín García, sir—listener."

"Um . . . I beg pardon?"

"That's quite all right, sir."

Mairena was forced to lash out at the uproar among the class jokers produced by this little exchange.

"There is no reason to laugh, friends, and less still for ridicule. True enough, I avoid categorizing students—registered, special, matriculated, unmatriculated—and I happily dispense with platforms, cathedra, and all the rest of it as teacher (As a rule Mairena taught without props, on his feet). We all chat Socratically here: sometimes affably and sometimes in heated discussion. That is all to the good, I would say. However, somebody must listen! So go on cultivating your specialty, Mr. García."

Dialectic according to Martínez

"Seeing his nakedness in the mirror of the waters," said Mairena, launching an exercise in rhetoric, "man said to himself: 'Here is something utterly beautiful that should be carefully safeguarded.' Then he invented his clothing. For obviously —Take it from there, Mr. Martínez, enlarge on the theme."

"For obviously," said Martínez, "obviously, sir . . ."

"Yes, Mr. Martínez . . ."

"Obviously, sir, all clothing presupposes a prior condition of nakedness. Right, sir?"

"Keep talking, Mr. Martínez."

"Er . . . clothes presuppose nudity—a prior condition of nudity. The function of clothing, first of all, is to safeguard and protect our corporeal nakedness; and second of all, to assure, beyond all manner of doubt, the possibility of later unclothing. Does that check, sir?"

"Not a doubt of it."

"In the same way, for the same or similar reasons, cages were invented to safeguard and assure the free flight of birds. For obviously . . ."

"Keep talking, Mr. Martínez."

"Well, bird cages, properly speaking, presuppose a prior option of flight. Weren't birds the inventors of bird cages after all? Obviously so. It is perfectly clear that without a prior option of flight, bird cages would have never existed."

Voice: "Certainly! Certainly!"

"Certainly. It follows, does it not, that just as our clothes owe their existence to a primal condition of nakedness, cages owe their existence to a primal prerogative of flight. Equally, just as partisans of clothing are not necessarily enemies of nudity but rather its loyal retainers, the proponents of bird cages can hardly be called implacable foes of free flight."

Voice: "Certainly! Certainly!"

Second voice: "Pray, what's so certain?"

"Nothing is certain, if you fail to give it some thought. There is (1) a nudity *ante indumentum,* which we bring into the world at our birth, like that of our first parents, when even the impulse to clothe ourselves has never suggested itself, much less to unclothe ourselves! (2) There is a nudity coeval with clothing, which relates more or less to the shame of our nakedness or to meteorological qualms about weather. (3) There is, finally, the nudity *post indumentum,* the nudism practised by nudists, who could never have imagined their nudity without the prior existence of clothes. Do I make myself clear, sir? If so, may I go on with a question? What have nudists got against clothing, sir? Clothes, after all, make their nudity possible: they safeguard our nakedness, protect and encourage the wish to go naked, and contribute in the long run to the attainment of that wish. Am I getting anywhere, sir?"

"Keep talking, Mr. Martínez."

"And why should the friends of free flight deplore the existence of cages? Bird watchers, I mean, or the birds themselves for that matter? There is a natural condition of free flight, like paradisiacal nakedness, that cages in no way impair, preëmpt, or diminish; there is also a flight coeval with cages—caged flying, as it were, sir—the freedom to fly, inside the bird cage itself, toward any point of the compass. No one would deny, of course, that this kind of flight has lost its first innocence. On the other hand, it has gained the noblest of all goals: the wish to fly out of its cage. But cages, it will be argued, are a constant obstacle to that goal. Obviously so. Nevertheless, they remain the *conditio sine qua non* for the ultimate attainment of that goal. For how could a bird fly out of its cage if bird cages never existed?"

"That's quite enough, Mr. Martínez. You have utterly persuaded us. And what is the title of your little dissertation?"

"'*On Nudity and Liberty, Properly Understood,*' sir."

¶ I note with some satisfaction, Mairena remarked to his students, that our class time in sophistry has not been utterly wasted. Through the use—and abuse, some would say—of old-fashioned logic, we have hit on a concept of things properly understood that should furnish a point of departure for future attempts to understand things better. That is the spectrum of our cumulative understanding: first, to understand things, or believe that we do; second, to understand things well; third, to understand them better; fourth, to understand there is no way of understanding them better without first improving the caliber of our head pieces. When we come to understand that much, circumstances will be propitious for better understanding; or rather, we will have reached the threshold of philosophy itself, where I would have to abandon you, for unregenerate rhetoricians like myself are forbidden to cross over that threshold.

XXVII

¶ Of all Spanish romantics, Mairena said to his students, I choose Espronceda.* Not that I consider him the purest romantic of all, but because in my opinion it was this dandy from Almendralejo who planted romanticism deepest into our Spanish entrails—actually played on the strings of our cynical (not our stoical) heritage with his romantic and languishing fingers. He touched the demoniacal quick of our great Spanish people, where, as is well known to folklorists, the profoundest blasphemies thrive.

The writings of Espronceda and the anecdotes concerning his life reveal a cynic in the full license of that word: an imperfect Socratic, in whom the cult of the good and the true merges with a compulsion to empty his bowels on all that our brooms have swept cleanest, to put it crassly. It seems that in a Christian atmosphere the cynic always ends up in blasphemy, whereas his confrere the stoic stops short, either on principle or through the saving grace of humor.

In Espronceda we have our most powerful poet of cynical inspiration, one whose vigor still serves to ensure the creativity of Spanish poetry. Read, I beg you, his masterpiece *The Student from Salamanca.* I read it as a boy—at an age when one should read most things, really—and have never had to reread it to evoke its total force at will, chiefly through the fascination of a few lines like:

> I have hurled back my soul . . .

A great—a very great—poet, and we have in his Don Félix de Montemar the synthesis or, better still, a Spanish epitome of all the Don Juans. After Espronceda there is the lovely page in Baudelaire that Espronceda would never have scrupled to take for his own, so closely does it match the spirit of his Don Félix,

*José de Espronceda (1808–1842). Poet and revolutionary, Byronic in his art as in his life. Author of *El estudiante de Salamanca,* a poem in four parts and a variety of meters, dealing with the dissolute Don Félix de Montemar, "second Don Juan Tenorio."

as epilogue or ornamental *ex libris* to *The Student from Salamanca:*

Quand Don Juan descendit vers l'onde souterraine . . .

❡ Let us not delude ourselves. Our passion for the country is a mere penchant for landscape, for nature as spectacle. There is nothing less rustic—or, if it comes to that, less "natural"—than a landscape enthusiast. After Jean Jacques Rousseau, that city-surfeited Genevan, the bucolic sensibility, the essentially georgic, with its emphasis on the plowing and planting of land, the Virgilian theme, and even that of our Lope, disappeared. The meadows of modern art are an invention of the city, an outcome of citified ennui and our growing terror of human agglomeration.

Love of nature? Possibly. Modern man roots in the countryside in search of his solitude—a highly unnatural quest. Others contend he is really in search of himself. But our natural bent is to look for ourselves in those closest to us—in our neighbor, as Unamuno, the sapient young rector of Salamanca has put it. For my own part, I am convinced modern man is in flight from himself, that he takes to the plants and the boulders in disgust at his own animality, which our cities corrupt and exacerbate. Physicians have a quaint way of putting it: he goes to the country for his health; and that, once understood, says it all.

XXVIII

℄ You have probably noted, Mairena observed to his students, that I rarely press moral considerations (that preserve of all rhetorists par excellence!). I must admit to you now that morality was never my forte. Not, I hasten to add, because I am a man "beyond good and evil," like certain readers of Nietzsche: there, my moral concern, like Nietzsche's, would be a crucial consideration, but for exactly the opposite reason: that I have never, not even in my dreams, emerged from the maze of the good and the evil, the good and the bad—from that which, seeming good, might yet become better, and that which, seeming evil, might yet become worse. All vision requires a factor of removal, of perspective: there is no way of seeing things without first taking leave of them. That was Nietzsche's way of dealing with the moral, and for that reason alone he has passed on into history.

℄ My teacher had some local fame as a drunk, because on the solemn occasions of his lifetime—his betrothal, the awarding of his doctorate, competitive examinations for the chair—he reinforced his morale, as he put it, or foreshortened his sense of responsibility with frequent libations. The good people demurred: Faugh! a metaphysical babbler, smelling of brandy—scandalous! Imagine how he puts it away outside the classroom! Truth to tell, he took to the bottle on only these solemn occasions. However, he made no move to quash all the sinister rumors, for a number of reasons that recommended themselves to his judgment. First, because alcohol, as he said, "is a part of my legend, and without a legend, no one passes into history." Second, "because scholars to come would need something to verify apart from the drearily literary." Third, "out of gratitude to alcohol as such, which has often helped me over many a hump." Fourth, "out of regard for those good nonabstainers, who proudly number me among the saturated." Fifth, "because my aridity is hardly so moisture-proof I can boast about it." Sixth, "because, in the final analysis, the absence of vices adds so little to the sum of one's virtues."

¶ We must each say the best that we can for ourselves and serve notice on our neighbor accordingly. Should you happen to grasp something I've said, rest assured, friend, I understand matters differently!

XXIX

❡ I have always tabled discussions of *amor* as something essentially poetic, and therefore outside the scope of this course; and in another sense, because no theme has more consistently taxed and abused the resources of rhetoric. Further, the theme is becoming too scabrous for pedagogical use, knotted and twisted as it is by science, and augmented by psychiatrists who have brought forth any number of disagreeable matters never dreamt of in our philosophies, along with a glossary of terms to define and canonize them. Further, many women and some men confess themselves not only to priests but to medical specialists as well; thus they have duplicated the arcana of love, on one hand, and its cunning, on the other—and added to the documentary treasures of erotica, on the third hand.

❡ Our cultural accumulation of data from the specialized sciences has become, despite all its advantages, something fearsome: no one can now sum up the fund of existing knowledge, though we all know that in each thing there is always "somebody in the know." Our awareness of our shortcomings either forces us into silence or turns us into pedants: into people talking without knowing what they are saying about what others presumably know. Thus the sum of our learning, no longer wholly in the keeping of anybody, adds appallingly to the volume of our conscious self-ignorance. Everything considered, one thing is about as urgent as another. I confess I have no notion what a latter-day Socrates would say to all this, or where the gravity of his irony would fall, or how we could ever profit by his maieutical skills.

❡ The cardinal sin, my teacher Abel Martín used to say, that a people can never condone is the sin attributed, rightly or wrongly, to Socrates: that he introduced new gods. Any new gods in the pantheon will of course include a number of the old, more or less decorously pensioned off. But the ancient vendetta against new gods, either actual or imagined, is understandable, since no novelty is more terrible in its consequences. Men have always suspected somehow that without a changing of the gods all will remain approximately as before, and that everything changes catastrophically when the gods themselves change.

ℭ But gods change of themselves, without any possibility of our altering matters: they affirm themselves, themselves, despite all that my teacher (who boasted of introducing his own god) believed. Our only recourse is to see them as they are, when they come, naked and unmasked. It will never do to say of the gods, as one says of God: those who look upon His Face shall perish! The gods walk with us, into our lifetimes; knowing them, we walk among gods. They abandon us silently at the doorsill of death, which perhaps they never cross over. We must labor to deserve the imperturbable gift of their pathos, which the Greeks knew so well how to cut on their funerary stele.

ℭ Sometimes the senile have the venerable look one recalls in Virgil's verses to Charon:

> jam senior, sed cruda deo viridisque senectu.

If my Latin were handier, we could go into that further, as the lines themselves deserve, in that magnificent language for senators. However, ancients of this kidney are not too abundant; nature does not seem to take oldsters so seriously. The seedy old boy, the dotty old duffer, and the self-serving old bore are better known to us—hardworking comedians waving their batons in their fists on the podiums of the orchestras of this world.

XXX

℃ The only living language is the language in which we think and have our being. We are given only one—not always the tongue we are born to: we must content ourselves with the surfaces, grammatical and literary, of all the others. There is no need to insist that the young learn to speak any language but their native Castilian, the imperial tongue of their country. The study of French or Italian or German or English should be pursued like the study of Latin and Greek: without conversational intent. A Spanish *causeur* among cultivated Frenchmen would be something utterly asinine; returning to Spain with the passing of years, he would find himself disoriented and deprived by the difficulty of thinking clearly in two different tongues. Heaven preserve us from those who seek to render into their own language the utter inconsequence they necessarily think in another! And if one of them should turn statesman . . .

Those were my teacher's sentiments, a somewhat reactionary soul, I suppose, and by no means a model of consistency, since, on the other hand, he detested the professional purists of his own country—most of all, those out of Valladolid.

℃ No one need fear for his thoughts, however much his thinking may seem to run counter to basic procedures of logic. All things possible to thought need to be thought through by somebody, and the realist's stance may well be the crowning folly of them all. That two and two inevitably make four is a notion common to many. But those who think otherwise should take pains to say so. Nothing should be too outlandish. Nor should we insist on subsequent proof of such assertions; that would be tantamount to imposing the norms of our own mental processes on other minds, forcing them to concoct rationales in our image for the purpose of convincing us. Such norms and polemical tactics confirm nothing but our own suppositions—never the suppositions of others. When one has attained to this perfect disparity of working assumptions, the *onus probandi* is really nobody's responsibility.

℄ That painter—that really very breathtaking painter*—who sees the living as dead and inanimate things as alive, paints for our pleasure a craggy company of men seated at a marble table around a glimmer of bottles and glasses and cups that seem charged with the oddest uneasiness—as if at any moment they might blow up in smithereens and bury themselves in the rafters. As a painter he sees life where none of the rest of us sees it, and understands, as we never shall, the death that we carry inside us. The result is sheer genius: he sees objects as we can not, and compels us to see them as he does. To weary him with proofs and demonstrations that a man is always more vital than a siphon of seltzer water, or to engage him to show us the contrary, would be utterly beside his purposes and ours.

℄ That existence cannot be deduced from essence is to many an established fact, after Kant; and that essence is not necessarily deducible from existence—what being is—assuming it to be something—is equally apparent to those who hold that the spatiotemporal world is a world of mere appearance. If we explore those two complementary positions, so open to dispute on all levels, we must soon run head-on into the unshakable faith of human reason: faith in the void and the word.

Where are we going, we poet-apprentices committed to reason's nihilist faith, at the bottom of the barrel of our consciousness? There are those who maintain that the poet is a type of the ingenuous man, disengaged from all metaphysical dilemmas, and should remain so. That might very well serve, were it not for the fact that our human ingenuousness is precisely what poses such problems.

℄ My teacher maintained, Mairena went on, that the basis of

*José Gutiérrez Solana (1881–1952). Painter of grotesque and dramatic inspiration.

consciousness could never be the nihilistic faith of our reason, and that reason itself, working in nihilist faith, has not said the last word. His philosophy, which was really a meditation on the work of the poet, led him to wholly different conclusions and convictions than those mentioned above. He believed that all poetry—even the most negative and saturnine—is always an act of clairvoyance: an affirmation of absolute realities, since poets always believed what they saw, regardless of the eyes they elected to see through as poet and as man. Vital experience—have we any other that matters?—has taught man that life is impossible without vision, that vision alone constitutes evidence, that people never doubt what they *see;* they only doubt what they *think.* The task of the poet, he added, is to break the dialectical bounds of the spirit—the intransigently skeptical spirit; he must understand that he has been brooding on Nothingness, distracted for a while by the bone given him to gnaw by the gods, as a pastime to cheat metaphysical hunger.

My teacher tried to put it in terms of fantasy and myth:

> And God said: "Let Nothing come forth!"
> And He raised His right hand
> to blot out the sight from His vision. And
> Nothing came forth upon earth.

XXXI

❨ *Mairena begins to expound the poetics of his teacher, Abel Martín*

My teacher used to say: It is evident—when he said "evident," he was never sure of himself, or suspected others of holding contrary positions—it is evident that all human reason militates against the diversity and richness of things; that it anxiously roots for a unifying principle, a something to explain all things, in order to abide by that something and lighten the burden and bedlam of all the other things. Thus, on one hand, we have rational faith, faith in the always unseen—the being of things, their essence, their substance, their primordial stuff, call it what you will; and on the other hand, there is that great hamper of particolored scraps, into which tumbles the whole world of appearances, and within it the heart of humanity. And even if we attribute the pull of our rational faith to the magnet of pure Nothingness, while reason misses its mark, with no shred of gratuitous truth to support it—still its annihilating force, the disintegrative power of reason, is an omen to keep us bemused. Marvel and miracle: that power of thought to cut through the wilderness tangle of our senses, as if no jungle were there, and evoke, on the site of the jungle itself, the great void! Yet even to envision man's intellect, for graphic effect, as an ax hacking paths through a forest misses some of the miracle; for the felled tree and the ax leave the woodland intact, but the cut of the mind is another thing. As poets, the whole prodigy of thinking concerns us: the great egg of the cosmos, emptying and filling itself—and all, as they say, in the flutter of an eyelid.

❨ But the poet must keep a respectful distance from the philosopher, from the purely contemplative man concerned with the posing and methodical exposition of the great problems of thought. The poet's is a household variety of metaphysics; by which I mean the inevitable poem of his ultimate beliefs, the whole of his radical wonder. The poetical character—*on poetikos*—does not pose any problems for the poet; it only veils or discloses itself, and wherever it discloses itself there it is. The poet's relation to Nothingness, to *Nada,* on the other hand, is another thing: there he questions. "What is it? Who made it? How was it made? When was it made? For whom was it made?" And a whole flood of questions that have gathered and bulked with the years, and have their source in the mind and passions of the poet. For Nothingness, as I have often remarked, is always an agon, an anguish; but for poets, above all other things, it is also a perennial source of admiration and awe.

℄ The purely logical, or the *reductio ad absurdum* of pure logic, was one of the roads by which my teacher arrived at that great awe of *Nada* so essential to his poetics. The Great Nothing overawes us (*nos asombra*), said my teacher, with a passing play on words, rather than overwhelms us (*nos ensombrece*); it is given us there to rejoice in the shadow of God's hand and reflect in the cool of His being, rather than drowse off in that presence, as certain sinister mystical cults, justly condemned by the Church, have sometimes yearned to do.

℄ Before it be Day if day be given, indeed,
when under Thy shadowing hand, I sleep sound . . .

Thus my teacher sought to express, not a hope or a desire, but a dread: the dread of "dying the death," of being wholly expunged from eventual illumination by the hand of his God. For my poor teacher suffered agonies—painful, exhausting, vexatious—the true death draft of Manrique, doubting his lifetime's poetics:

Before it be Day, if day be given, indeed,
the all-beholding light, that is not yet come to pass . . .

The Buddhist's nirvana was more native to him than the paradisiacal hopes of the just: in truth, he was an habitual blasphemer. Nonetheless he must have found salvation of a sort in the end, judging by the terminal act of his anguish, which was literally the act of drinking death down without too much ado.

℄ But whether "Day be given" or not—with or without a capital D—this much is certain: all that is problematic in being as such is the offspring of Nada; we must go on from that point to reckon and build with it further. Deep and early she planted herself in our souls, and hardly a memory of childhood escaped her.

XXXII

(Cleanse your spirit of spleen, my teacher said, before exercising your function as critics. Not that the voiding of spleen doesn't pose certain dangers: there are some souls who have nothing else to offer, who run the risk of blanking themselves out with purgation. "Be pure, be pure, and evermore be pure: but be not too pure," for we live in essential impurity. Melancholia, black bile—*atra bilis*—has joined with the poet more than once to produce imperishable pages. There is no need to begrudge the critic a little melancholy. Nonetheless, a little soap here, a little swab there have their place in the household of literature.

(Re intimate diaries, my teacher said, was anything ever less intimate?

(*Kant and Velázquez*

It is evident, my teacher used to say—Mairena had a way of relegating all responsibility for evidence to his teacher—it is evident that if Kant had been a painter, he would have painted something very like Velázquez' *Young Maids in Waiting;* and a little judicious reflection on that painting by the celebrated master of Seville will lead us straight to the *Critique of Pure Reason,* the luminous classic by the master from Königsberg. While the French were producing their Descartes, we came forth—though some still deny our modernity—with nothing less than a Kantian painter, untouched by romantic excess. That is saying a very great deal; I therefore say nothing of the extravagant comparisons put forth by others—Marx as Christ, for example—which apparently astonish nobody. If it so happens I have grossly misinterpreted the stars, Kant, as it luckily turns out, was never really a painter nor Velázquez a philosopher.

We can agree on one point: Velázquez, so little attracted to sensible forms—judging by his indifference to the beauty of his sitters—could hardly have held an esthetic other than the transcendental esthetic of Kant. Probe for another as you please: you will never find any. His realism, so completely divorced from naturalism—by which I mean the penchant for wallowing blissfully in the dungheap of the actual—is that of a man who has swallowed down his metaphysics and tells us, with *that* in his belly: "Painting exists!" as Kant might have said: "Here is physico-mathematical science: a staggering fact that admits of no doubt." Since that time, to paint has been to fix upon canvas precisely the forms that the spirit contrives out of chromatic and luminous matter, in an enchanted cage of space and time. And all this, needless to say, "spoken" with a brush!

That is the secret of the calm magnificence of Velázquez. He paints *through* all, *for* all men; his pictures are not merely *paintings,* but *painting.* Speaking of Velázquez—not always with the awe due him—some have found fault, more or less surreptitiously, with his impassive objectivity. They would even imply by that word—think of it!—the objective of the photographer's camera. How soon they forget, said my teacher, that objectivity, in any sense of the word, is a miraculous achievement of the human spirit. Its delights are open to all, but to suspend it in space, in stone or on canvas—that is always a labor for titans.

ℂ *On the novel*

What really makes the reading of some novels, and the conversation of most women, a trial is their insipid penchant for anecdote, insignificant detail, unvarnished documentation, with no hint of extension imaginative, reflective, or esthetic. The urge to tell all, down to the last dropping of doorkeeper's gossip! All that overballast to shipwreck the mariner, while we wallow in the sea of the temporal! The pity of it is that with it we forfeit certain turns of expression we might have saved from oblivion, certain oddments of observation, profound and original reflections that abound in this kind of novel. And surely, a little rhetorical play, as we have come to understand it, is in order.

❡ It is very possible that the modern novel has not yet discovered its metier, the sure line of its contour. Perhaps, in the clutter of documents, it has lost its heuristic initiative. On the whole, it is an ill-defined genre, more didactic than poetic in character. It is a milieu for bricklayers, rather than architects and, as such, runs the risk of caving in at the sides before the roof beams are properly in place.

❡ *Cervantes*

Our Cervantes, Mairena continued to his students, never murdered the knightly romances, which were as good as dead when he found them; he gave them a habitation and a life in the brain cells of a madman, as mirages of the deserts of La Mancha. Out of these very same chronicles of chivalry, degenerate epics—these novels, properly speaking—he created the novel for moderns. Out of that lowliest gambit of literature, the pastiche—here is the irony!—the most original work in any literature emerged. No one can ever deprive us as Spaniards of this glory: for all that is ours—most deeply our own—resembles nothing else in the world.

A strange and a marvelous world, that world of the Cervantine fiction, with its double time and its double space, and its twinned series of figures—real and hallucinatory—two exemplary monads, like wide-open windows, two integral, complementary consciousnesses, conversing and forging ahead! Opposing, with Plato and Christ, the incurable sophistry of human reason, the *solus ipse* of things, the humor of Cervantes presses forward, a book of harlequinade, creating a spiritual climate which is ours to this day. It will be long, very long, before we shall look upon its like again.

XXXIII

℄ *Mairena talking, not always infallibly*

Under all that we think, lives all we believe, like the ultimate veil of our spirits. There are people so profoundly divided in themselves that they believe the contrary of what they think. I dare say they are the most common. Politicians should bear this in mind. What they call opinion is a more complex and equivocal phenomenon than they think. At moments of massive upheaval that rock the conscience of peoples to their depth, strange prodigies are at work, elusive and hard to assess: sudden conversions, attributed to self-interest; unforeseeable changes of heart, called insincere; inexplicable stances. What is really taking place is a showing forth of latent opinion, the hidden world of commitment at the bottom of the barrel of our consciousness.

Political frivolity is known by its total ignorance of these phenomena. The great debacles of history serve us best by forcing us to see such phenomena clearly, with a gravity not possible when all we have eyes for is a ripple agitating the surface.

℄ *In the café*

"From a certain point of view, my teacher once said, there is nothing more bourgeois than a proletarian—which is hardly very strange, since the proletariat is a creation of the bourgeoisie. The proletariat of the world, he went on, are joined in a common mission to liquidate the bourgeoisie with all possible dispatch; and thereafter, themselves."

"Your teacher, my dear Mairena, was mad as a March hare."

"Possibly so. But listen here, Tortolez, my friend: I have a little story to tell you: about an Andalusian candy maker—an agnostic, as a matter of fact; a philosophical pragmatist set out to convert him to the religion of his ancestors."

"*His* ancestors? Whose ancestors, Mairena, my friend? The 'his' is rather amphibolic."

"The ancestors of the philosophical pragmatist, very likely. But listen to what the philosopher told him: 'If you put your faith in God, in a Supreme Judge who exacts a full reckoning for your actions, you would make much finer candies than those you now offer for sale, come down on your prices, and go up on your profits, since your custom would be vastly increased. You should really believe in a deity.' 'But does God really exist, esteemed doctor?' the candy man asked. 'The question is trivial,' the philosopher told him. 'All that matters is that you believe He exists.' 'And what if I cannot?' the candy man asked him again. 'That is equally beside the point: it is enough that you *wish* to believe. That way three things can happen: either you begin to believe just a little; or to believe you believe, which comes to the same thing, practically; or, at the very least, you can turn out fine candies just as though you really believed. The result would be exactly the same: you improve the quality of your merchandise in your own interest, and that of your clients.'"

"The candy man," my teacher went on, "was by no means unimpressed by the philosopher's reasoning. 'Come back a few days from now,' he said."

"When the philosopher returned, he found that the candy man had put out a new shingle: *Sweetshop of Ángel Martínez, Caterer to His Divine Majesty.*"

"Very edifying. But tell me, Mairena, old friend: did the quality of his candy . . ."

"The quality of his candy did not improve in the slightest. But what the candy man said to his philosopher-friend is this: 'All that matters is that you believe they are better; or that you wish to believe they are better; or, at the very least, that you eat the candy and pay me cold cash just as though you believed.'"

XXXIV

¶ *On the unlikely collapse of a League of Nations*

Some day, Mairena observed in a café, all the great powers will convene to assure peace in our time. Will they get it? That is a horse of a different color! One thing is certain, however: the prestige of the League could never thereafter be impugned. If a conflict of small nations should arise, the great powers will paternalistically cry: Peace! If the small fry should then come to blows, no one will stop them. The big fellows will say: We can hardly afford to involve ourselves in this sort of thing, or convert a trivial spat between pygmies into a major engagement for titans. Though we cannot maintain absolute peace in the world, the League will at least keep wars limited: and so their prestige would be saved. And if a conflict arose among the great powers themselves, the League would very probably vote itself out of existence: and a nonexistent League can hardly be said to collapse.

"And what if a great nation should set out to snap up a small one, Mairena my friend? What do the associated great powers do then?"

"Stand shoulder to shoulder in the passes to frustrate the enemy, my dear Don Cosme."

"And if the great power insisted on devouring the little one?"

"Then the other great powers will solemnly enjoin it to do so, in the name of them all. And still the prestige of the League would be saved."

¶ The spiritual grace of the great Spaniard* lost to us today deserves something more than a niche in the ethopoeic succession of ordinary Spanish accomplishment. Hardly a portrait is left us that does him justice. The most acceptable, the work of an artist from Valencia, faithfully transcribes the refinements of his physical person but nothing more. The expression is blunder-

*Francisco Giner de los Ríos (?).

ing and ineffectual, as though the hand of the painter still groped for a means of resolutely engaging that inner authority—unmarred by the slightest suggestion of pretension—we all came to see in him. The closest we can come to a likeness, it may be, is the figure of the Marquis de Espinola receiving the keys to the conquered city, in Velázquez' portrait by that name. For the general depicted there seems to have triumphed by a twofold exertion of spirit and intelligence—to have understood fully that yesterday's triumph may well prove tomorrow's defeat; and he would know how to lose everything with identical elegance of spirit. So much Velázquez, that prince among painters, caught with his brush: the chivalry of triumph unsullied by vainglory—something at once Castilian and deep in the Spanish grain itself, part of the essence of the man whose passing we lament today. It is right and expedient that we mourn him without stint or reservation, in the spirit of Shakespeare's speech for the grieving Romans on the occasion of Caesar's death: ". . . you are not stones, but men." And to our spirit's bereavement we may even add a touch of that forgetfulness which refines all we remember.

¶ The day may yet come, Mairena says to his students, when the poets will change places with the philosophers. The poets will sing of their wonderment in the presence of the great metaphysical adventure, especially that supremest of all marvels: the power of contemplating being untrammeled by time, essence disengaged from existence—the fish in his element and out of it, as it were, viewing the very waters of the river as an illusion of fish. They will deck their lutes with garlands and chant the old miracles of human meditation.

The philosophers, on the other hand, pondering like poets the *fugit irreparabile tempus,* will gradually muffle their viols with veils. And out of that romantic deviation, an existentialist metaphysics will emerge rooted deeply in time: something, in fact, more poetic than philosophical in character. For the philosophers will speak to us of our anguish, the essentially poetical anguish of being, face to face with nonentity (*la nada*); while the poets will appear drunken with radiance, reeling under the old, Eleatic superlatives. Thus poet and philosopher will confront each other, no longer enemies, each carrying forward the great labor where it is relinquished by the other.

So spoke Mairena, anticipating, albeit vaguely, the vision of a poet, à la Paul Valéry, and a philosopher, à la Martin Heidegger.

XXXV

℄ Juan de Mairena had long cherished the idea of founding on his native soil a popular school of wisdom. He abandoned the project only with the death of his teacher, for whom he had destined the chair of poetics and metaphysics. The chair of sophistry he had reserved for himself.

The pity of it, he said, is that our best-laid plans are always the first to miscarry, while the vagaries of fools, meddlers, and charlatans prosper to the end. Ours is a people gifted with a marvelous capacity for wisdom in the loftiest sense of the word: a folk not yet addled by a middle class distracted in its turn by the scientific indigence of our universities and the pragmatism of our clergy—that inveterate stumbling block of all high spiritual exertion. As a rule, we insist on teaching the rank and file how to read without specifying in advance the purposes to be served or realizing how deeply they suspect the paucity of our own reading. We assume they will come to thank us one day for the "practical" schools where one learns the most scientific and time-saving techniques for driving a saw through a plank; and we innocently believe they would laugh in our faces at any mention of Plato. A grievous mistake! it is only the dandies of this world, in the worst sense of that word—if there is, indeed, a better!—who snicker when Plato is mentioned.

℄ Such a school would flourish in Spain, needless to say, only if there were teachers capable of implementing these aims—and nowhere more so than in Andalusia, where man has not yet been debased by a perverse mystique of hard work or, rather, a feverish pursuit of money for purchasing pleasures and material satisfactions in exchange for muscular exhaustion.

It was only natural, if I may be permitted a passing digression, that northern European man, originally charged with extracting and convoying the weight and the bulk of this world, a hacker of forests driven to brutal exertion in adverse climates of the globe, would seek emancipation in the machine; whereas the culture of the south, originally enslaving and serf-minded, would look to leisure as the *sine qua non* of the good life, striving ascetically to reduce to a minimum man's more or less bestial appetites.

In any event, my teacher went on, a sound concept of work would always look upon it as a marginal activity more or less kinesthetic in character, on the frontiers and in the service of the more specifically human activities: attention, reflection, speculation, sympathetic contemplation, and so on—all essentially quietistic or, to put it more modestly, sedentary pursuits. But let us defer for a later time any further talk of my teacher and his theories, now a little musty, concerning *Homo sapiens* as opposed to *Homo faber*, or his more quixotical notion of a *Homunculus mobilis* turned pure projectile and forfeiting thereby his working animality. Let us turn again to the school of wisdom.

¶ For a project of this sort, Mairena went on to explain, the extraordinary man, rather than a working exemplar of our species, would be required; not, however, a teacher in the manner of Zarathustra, whose ethicobiological insolence none of us could endure for even a fortnight. Rather let us have a man in the traditional line of Protagoro-Socratico-Platonism as it intersects with Christianity. For it could never be the intent of our school to erect a new scholasticism postulating a Church and a political power more or less committed to the defense and patronage of a dogma with all its attendant tabus: quite the contrary. Our man must have nothing whatever of the sacerdotal about him, or the propitiator, or the catechist, just as his pupils must utterly eschew the aura of the sectarian, the parochial, and the catechumen. Ours would be a Delphic order of aphorism translated into the vulgate of the Romance languages in suasive rather than categorical terms: "It behooves thee to strive after . . ." And we would add: "Let no one enter here who presumes to know anything about anything"—not even geometry, which we would probably study as an essentially inexact science. For the keystone of our school, with its two founding chairs like the two blades of a single shears—the chairs of sophistry and metaphysics—would be to reveal to a people, namely, the folk of our native soil, the whole ambiance of their possible thought, the length and the breadth of those vast zones where the spirit is alternately illumined and darkened; to induce them to recontemplate the already contemplated, to un-know the already known and doubt what they already hold in doubt: for that is the only way we can begin to believe in anything.

XXXVI

☾ *Other aspects of the school of wisdom*

The historical religions, Mairena observes to his students, so-called "revealed," would have nothing whatever to fear from our school of wisdom; for it would be our task not to discredit existing faiths but to concentrate on a quest for the sum of our own belief. Only the pseudo-beliefs would be open to our attack (not always openly): unbelief in the guise of avowed belief. "You there, for instance, Mr. Martínez."

"Present!"

"You could carry your expectations of hell-fire and damnation to whatever well-roasted extremes you prefer; but you may not with propriety enjoin them upon your neighbor without decisive prior participation in them as acts of faith. I wonder if you understand me correctly. There is only one religion which we denounce as irreligious and oppose with all our force: the supine and perverse cult which debases all Western thinking. We name it after the fashion of the Anglo-Saxons of the New World, who still call the tunes, 'pragmatism': that is how we baptize an ingenious philosophy—or, rather, an ingenious want of philosophy. The word itself may be a little too constricted for our intended meaning, for we would want it to include the 'natural religion' which scoundrels the world over share in common. Our hope would be to assist, with all the power at our command, in cleansing the world of hypocrisy and the cant of the Englishman."

☾ Surely, my teacher prophetically declared, we are on the eve of great blood baths and implacable revolutions whose sources go back, it may be, to some discordancy between action and the postulated ideals of action: a massive contest between all that we hold elemental and an order of life which would inundate us in a tidal wave of cynicism. We are hastening a gigantic moral catastrophe in which only the cynical virtues will emerge unscathed. Politicians, if they are to govern at all, will have to persist in their cynicism and govern by its aid. Let it be our mission to seize the initiative by the exercise of intelligence which confers upon the human animal the dignity of men. That is the most profoundly didactic aspect of our Popular School of Higher Wisdom.

ℭ We would never presume to "educate the masses"—Devil take the "masses"! Our concern is properly with *man*, for man alone interests us: man in every sense the word has come to assume; man *in genere*, and man in his single identity; essential and empirical man viewed in the context of his place and his time, not excluding the human animal in his exigent relations with nature. But man in the mass has no meaning for us. Notions of mass relate only to distinctions of volume and bulk, and can never assist in the just definition of a man, for concepts of mathematical physics are notoriously devoid of humanity. Forgive me for laboring such truisms, but all must be spelled out in detail these days. Even those who would defend human agglomeration against the hateful exploiters of mankind seize upon the concept of mass and convert it into social, ethical, and even esthetic categories. The absurdity of it! Imagine what a pedagogy for the "masses" would let loose upon us! The education of the "child mass!" That would be a pedagogy for Herod himself—a monstrosity.

ℭ You are already aware, Mairena goes on to tell his pupils, of my scant enthusiasm for bullfights. I confess they have never entertained me. To be perfectly truthful, it is not in the nature of such occasions to entertain me; and I greatly suspect they have never really entertained anybody, for the spectacle they provide is far too somber for entertainment. The bullfight is not a game, a simulacrum more or less spirited or insipid in character, a lavish activity like the games of children or the gymnastics of their elders; it is not a useful exertion, like the braining of beeves in the slaughterhouse; much less an art, since it involves nothing of the fictive or the imagined. The bullfight is essentially a sacrifice. One does not play games with a bull if the aim is to kill it to no useful end—like offering it reverentially in a holocaust to an ineffable god. That is why, in my view of things, bullfights, though they entertain nobody, intrigue and inflame many. The taurine *afición* is in essence a Passion; or perhaps it would be truer to speak of a taurine fervor, since the Passion, properly speaking, is wholly the bull's.

❡ In our Popular School of Higher Wisdom we would have to deal at some point with the theme of tauromachia, so close to us all—to yourselves, primarily—and at the same time so curiously remote! Though I should be sorry to distress anyone, I must point out that it is precisely what is our own that baffles and mystifies us most. We have managed, to a degree I should never wish to deplore, to rid ourselves somewhat of the chauvinist's readiness to praise what is Spanish merely because it is Spanish. The chauvinist's stance is a polemical rather than a critical one, and I think we may claim it has never taken on the alarming proportions with us which it has in other countries of the world. It would be well for us never to adopt it again. However, a total absence of sympathy toward what is genuinely "ours" would have the opposite effect of gradually hobbling our spirits with a spurious critical apparatus we would one day have to consign to the attic with all the other outworn rubbish. In our Popular School of Higher Wisdom we would always be a little wary of the facile derogation of what is ours before coming closer to understand things better. For it is quite possible, I strongly suspect, that here with us in Spain many things are better in essence than they are in appearance—the inverse phenomenon of what we find elsewhere in the world; and that those who defile our heritage not only forfeit the possibility of understanding it but tempt us to self-loathing in the end.

❡ I have urged that we sometime give careful thought to bullfighting and to our afición for bulls, in particular. In so doing, we should avoid all inquiries into the origin and historical development of the fiesta—is it really a fiesta?—which we call "national" for want of a more adequate term. Our Popular School of Higher Wisdom would not serve as a center of historical investigation, despite our respect and esteem for centers serving such a function. Instead, we would have to ask ourselves as philosophers, men of a reflective discipline inquiring into the reasons for existing facts: what are bullfights, after all? What is the taurine afición—the excitement of the bloody spectacle wherein a man sacrifices a bull at the risk of life and limb? And a matador, gentlemen, a killer of bulls—the word has a solemn ring—who is not an arrant slaughterer—that least of all, surely!—or an executioner, or a dissembler of cruel rituals: what is such a matador, such a gallant and delicate swordsman, a nimble and vigorous immolator of brave bulls—bulls whom the circumstances of their sacrifice have made mad? If he is not a madman himself—for he seems to us not mad, but a discerning and knowledgeable man whose skills are never mastered till the first gray streaks his hair—is he, perhaps, a priest? Can he possibly appear in any other guise? What cultus of gods does he honor? That is the order of questions proper for our Popular School of Higher Wisdom.

XXXVII

ℭ *Juan de Mairena talks to his students*

The immutability of the past—*fugit irreparabile tempus*—a past which remains intact, inert, and unalterable, is a concept too firmly implanted in the human mind to be uprooted. How, indeed, could the machine of syllogistic procedure, which we must carry with us to the end, be expected to function without it? Our task in any class in sophistry in our Popular School of Higher Wisdom, Mairena tells his students, would be to inquire whether such a concept has any value apart from its logical usefulness, whether, so encumbered, we can ever pass on to a class in metaphysics. For the way beyond sophistry to metaphysics is one of ultimate beliefs and inevitable hypotheses which can resist every onslaught of implacable logic—a logic that does not balk at the suicidal to promulgate its resolute inanity.

Such a condition can come about only when, after prolonged and strenuous debate on any essential question, we arrive at an unalterable and illogical conclusion: namely, "There is no truth but death." That would be equivalent to asserting that all truth is nonexistent, and that this alone is the truth. In such a case it needs little further effort to understand we are still in the dark regarding the nature of the real truth, that logic at this point has abandoned all modes of judgment and rational inquiry. That is the triumph—a lamentable one, it may be, but none the less a triumph—of the skeptic, who, confronted with the *reductio ad absurdum* of his own theoretical reasoning, feels under no obligation to accept as true a contrary proposition which he initially refuted, choosing rather to discard as untenable the whole apparatus of logic.

ℭ *Mairena and the Generation of '98. A Nobel Prize*

When the first essays of Miguel de Unamuno appeared in print, there were many who said: "Here is Brand himself, Ibsen's Brand, transplanted from the Norwegian fjords to the uplands of Spain." Mairena put it another way: "Here is the great Spaniard so many have waited for. One of the sages, perhaps? Certainly that—a savant in the French sense of the word; but above all, a poetical watchmaker who has come to wind up our watches—or our souls—each stopped at its separate hour, and to regulate all time by the meridian of his people and his race. Later, it may be, they will all tick too fast or too slow again." Let us not press the image further.

℄ *The logic of Don Juan*

"Don Juan, I have come to kill you."

"In that case, you must be Don Luis."

Do you recall the scene in Act IV of *Don Juan Tenorio* of Zorrilla in which these verses occur? First Don Luis Mejía speaks, muffled in his cape, certain that he need not uncover in order to be identified. In view of Don Juan's little escapade with Doña Ana de Pantoja, we would have to admit that he can hardly say anything other than he says; but he could hardly have said it better. It would be difficult to imagine an answer more cynical or more serene—or more characteristic of that magnificent king of reprobates Don Juan Tenorio. "In *that* case . . ." Here is logic at its most felicitous. It is one instance among many where an acknowledged touchstone of theatrical eloquence achieves popular favor before it wins the esteem of the cultivated.

XXXVIII

℄ We may well find ourself in a social circumstance permeated throughout by a religious faith, on the one hand, and by a metaphysical faith which frankly runs counter to it, on the other. For example: for all our Christian faith—"manifest," like all others—in a paternal God who enjoins us to love His creation, of which we are part, without distinction or favor, there militates a metaphysical faith in the *solus ipse* that might be formulated in terms such as these: "Nothing exists in itself, except I as myself; the rest is mere representation, a figment of my spirit arrived at by subjective processes of thought, a simple contrivance to enact the will of the pure I, and so on." In short, just across the frontier of my selfhood, the kingdom of Non-Being (la Nada) begins. The heterogeneity of the two modes of belief neither excludes the possibility of their mutual contradiction nor admits of their reduction to a common denominator. And it is precisely in the realm of plain fact that conciliation founders. For the ethos of metaphysical belief is necessarily egocentric, self-loving. My *I* is capable of loving itself with an absolute love whose radius is infinite. But the love with which I love my neighbor—that other I which is never sufficient unto itself, that *I* represented by the absolute *I* of myself—can be given only lip service, at a remove. To such a pass of logic have we *enfants terribles*—and what else can we claim to be?—arrived! Bear in mind, too, that the formula of "Love thy neighbor as thyself; and do better than that, if necessary!"—the true creed of the Christian—implies a tenet of altruistic faith, a belief in the absolute reality of that other I as an existing entity in itself. If we are truly "children of God," God's noblemen—and that is the only basis for the modest pride in self which I have so frequently enjoined—how in the name of Christian faith may we then grossly and totally degrade our neighbor, strip him of his self-sufficiency, and convert him into a mere representation, a phantom of our own making?

℄ "And a sinister phantom, at that!" the least vocal member of the class dared to add in his turn.

"Who made that remark?" asked Mairena.

"Joaquin García, listener."

"Ah! you were saying . . ."

"A sinister phantom who may yet pay me back in my own coin. What I mean, sir, is: I would have to think of him as a product of my own fantasy who might one day convert me into a figment of *his* imagination."

"Capital, Mr. García, capital!" Mairena exclaimed. "You have given us an exact, if somewhat bizarre, definition of that other I who lives inside my *solus ipse:* 'a sinister phantom'—that is something really disquieting!"

XXXIX

¶ No one can charge us with having devoted our time to mundane or frivolous issues, among which I would include many matters reputed to be crucial, such as considerations of economics. Sometime, however, we must give them our attention—always taking care to elevate them to our special point of view. We shall have to ask ourselves some day whether the whole of the human species, of which we are only an insignificant part—all their nutritive and procreative drives—comprise a brute, categorical fact which needs no ethical justification; or whether, on the contrary, we must probe for the reasons behind such data and explore the metaphysical necessity underlying the categorical one. Are our lives regulated by laws or hard fact? Here is the crux of the issue. Let us understand it clearly: it is the ethical problem par excellence—a problem as old as mankind, which we must keep in the sharpest possible focus. For until it can be resolved, we shall never arrive at a working morality—that is to say, a configuration of norms for human behavior capable of persuading or constraining our neighbor. Meanwhile, it behooves us to leave room for the philanthropist, on the one hand, and the constabulary, on the other.

¶ Let us, said my teacher Abel Martín, imagine a non-Aristotelian theology which conceives of God as a great consciousness, of which our private consciousness is part—or into which, to transpose the image *grosso modo* to your range, our private consciousness has been telescoped. The indispensable adjunct to such a theology would be time: not mathematical, but physical time—a time coincident with that inchoate impatience which others have called anguish. In the stresses of that anguish we begin to catch intimations of the great nostalgia for non-being felt by the Supreme Being; or rather, the overpowering nostalgia of the One for the Other, as my teacher would say. To interpret His eternity in our terms and compensate for what might seem to be the less urgent business of moving the spheres, we would have to impose upon divinity an interminable labor—that of ceasing to be in His own right, of transforming Himself into the Other. "Has our listener something to say to that?"

"I find such a theology unacceptable," the listener observed. "I admit that a God who commits us to time and then removes Himself from it—or, to put it a little differently, remains quiescent Himself while moving our world for His diversion—is just as unacceptable. For if the world cannot move of itself, the most natural and feasible course would be to leave it alone, in its natural state. But the world is obviously in no need of a 'motor.' Up to this point we are in agreement. On the other hand, sir, a God totally immersed in time, obliged, like ourselves, to suffer it moment by moment, together with His awareness of that other 'interminable labor,' would be a God more unfortunate than His creation. He would be a poor devil of a God—to put it grossly—condemned to the galleys for a lifetime. Of course, sir, I can't say how far one is justified in talking of a God in these terms."

"To tell the truth," Mairena admitted uneasily, "there is something monstrous and repellent in pantheistic formulations of all sorts—though the metaphysic of my teacher was pantheistic in the extreme; the Church was right to condemn it through the ages. As I used to say to my teacher: many have fried in the fires of the Inquisition for far less reason! Fortunately, the Church is not inclined today to turn a serious ear to blasphemies against Aristotle. Still, I would urge you to reflect on this theme, lest you be caught off guard by a metaphysic from beyond which haunts our theology, a basically temporalist theology; and that in any event you find your own grounds for opposing or approving it, rather than live like perpetual monkeys in a world of the magic lantern, where questions of transcendency are concerned."

¶ I have said on occasion that I intend to avoid the pedantic. I went on, however, to make certain distinctions. I would like now to proceed to make others. How can the dedicated teacher escape the imputation of pedantry? Let us assume for the time being that only children are teachable, and that those who are capable of learning become as a child, even if they get to be as old as Methuselah. This much agreed, let us ask: How can a teacher—or a pedagogue, if you will—teach, educate, direct the thinking of children without transforming himself somewhat into a child in his turn and professing in the end a somewhat infantilized learning? For a teacher is to a certain degree the creation of the child. And it is infantilized learning, the infantile behavior of scholars, that is the identifying mark of the pedant, as the Greek etymology of the word itself would seem to suggest. Bear in mind also that the name pedant was originally applied to teachers who visited the homes of our grandfathers to instruct the young in grammar. Doubtless they cut a somewhat ridiculous figure; the very fact that they sought to teach the young something as remote from the thinking of children as grammar would indicate as much. Still, they were teachers and, as such merit our respect in the long run. The assumption that a teacher infantilizes himself—in a certain sense (*pais, paidos:* child) *pedanticizes* himself in his dealings with the young—should be carefully qualified. For whatever we propose to communicate to children we must first attempt to understand as children: and that is not the infantilism of a retarded mentality. In all the basic disciplines of study (poetry, logic, ethics) the infantilized view need never diminish the man. On the contrary, children demonstrate to us that almost all that eludes their understanding hardly merits teaching, and, above all, that when we ourselves falter as teachers, it is because we are imperfect in understanding.

XL

℄ Remember the verses in *Life Is a Dream** with which Clotaldo concludes his lengthy admonition of Rosaura and Clarín after surprising them in Segismundo's tower:

> Yield up your weapons and lives
> else this pistol of mine, this serpent
> of metal will spit forth
> its harrowing venom—
> two pellets, exploding, whose fires
> will outrage the air.

A modern adapter might be tempted to read it: "Hands up!" or "One move and I'll drill you!" in the belief that he had improved on the original and that his own theatrical pistol is more effective and terrifying than that of Calderón's old Cerberus. It is a debatable conclusion. For Calderón's Clotaldo seems to be as sure of his rhetoric as he is of his sidearms. As to the notion that it is the air that will be outraged . . . ! Our Clotaldo will bear watching! The true gunman is he who, like Clotaldo, need never pull the trigger.

℄ Of all man-made machines, the most interesting, in my judgment, is the watch, that specifically human artifact which animality alone could never have invented. The so-called *homo faber* would not deserve the title of *homo* but for his fabrication of watches. Yet the fact that he makes them is less important than the fact that he uses them; and more important still is the fact that he needs them. Man is the animal who must measure his time.

℄ Yes, man is the watch-using animal. My teacher let his own watch run down—he always carried a silver one—not long before he died, convinced that in the eternal life to which he aspired

---

**La vida es sueño*, dramatic masterwork of Pedro Calderón de la Barca (1600–1681).

it would be of little use to him; and that in the Nothingness into which he might well sink it would serve him not at all. What saddened him most was his conviction that but for his belief in death man would never have invented watches.

€ The watch in effect is proof indirect of man's belief in his mortality. For finite time alone can be measured: that much should be evident. However, we still have to ask ourselves why it is that man measures the short span allotted him. We know that time is measurable; but why seek to measure it? It is not enough to maintain that man measures time in order to make effective use of it, to order the activity of which it is full. That is a utilitarian rationale which tells us nothing as philosophers. Granted that we measure time in order to put it to use—what use does it serve? The implicit question remains unanswered: Why do we measure it? We are led to do so, in my judgment, by an illusion as old as the world itself: Zeno of Elea's belief in the infinitude of the finite, given its infinite divisibility. But the fleet-footed Achilles will never outdistance the tortoise, and the cunningly counted hour will never count itself out. From that point of view—the metaphysical, as always—the watch is a tool of sophistry, like any other.

XLI

℄ One of the infallible signs of a changing spiritual climate is our constant degradation of the comic and the concomitant brutalization of laughter. To tell the truth, there have never been so many good people abroad in the world whose laughter has the sound of an ass's bray.

℄ So much the better for us all, our progressivists would say! The ass's bray is a clear revelation of our waning comic absurdity. Seen at close range—or rather, heard at close range—there is nothing more mournful and in a way more apocalyptical than the bray of an ass.

℄ The cinema, my teacher often contended, to drive home a metaphysical point, is an invention of the Devil to bore the human species to distraction. It reveals the appalling esthetic fatuity of our essentially kinetic age, where man—that paragon of animals—betrays, in the guise of a work horse, the attributes of a mere projectile. For that creature outrageously racing down streets or shinnying up telegraph poles or showing himself on ledges and rooftops, only to plunge down a well, is as tedious in the long run as a cue ball made to ricochet on a billiard table. Until he is stopped in his tracks, I would think, we have no reason at all to be interested.

℄ None the less, in the motion picture, which has its own kind of artistry, like penmanship, or printing, or telegraphy—that is to say, not very much, and nothing that compares with its importance as a vehicle of culture and a medium for its diffusion—we have a right to expect that it align us with real objects, as photography does, with only the motion that is intrinsic to them rendered with the greatest possible exactitude. For in photography, only the real object, inexhaustible to those who know how to look at it, interests us. It should be enough that here in Chipiona we can view the cataracts of Niagara, canal boats on the Suez, and tuna fish in the hatcheries of Huelva. To photograph wraiths concocted in the studios of movie makers is an act of fantastic stupidity. The way to cheat the imagination of the imaginable is to give it to us outright in a photograph on a par with the perceivable objects of the real world. The child dreams in the imagery of the fairy tale only if he is allowed to imagine things for himself, or is left a margin for the imaginable. It is the same with adults. A photographed phantom is no more interesting than a coffeepot. Generally speaking, the cinema, oriented in part toward the novel, the anecdote, or the theater, is profoundly unedifying. It may addle us all by fostering a generation of moviegoers who are incapable of seeing and dreaming for themselves. When Europe falls to dictators with a scintilla of common sense, the jails will be flooded with movie makers.

ℂ *On politics*

Let us remember again the Machiavellian counsel which Machiavelli himself forgot: Order your lives so that your enemy is always in the wrong; give him no reasonable advantage over you. For man is an animal who attacks with his reason: I mean, he charges head-on with it. Heaven keep you from the impact of the brute primed with the charge of his reason!

ℂ *Juan de Mairena and the Generation of '98. Valle-Inclán*

Juan de Mairena's acquaintance with Valle-Inclán* dates to the year 1895; he heard from his own lips the whole story of the episode in Mexico, and was one of the three original purchasers of his first book, *Femininas.* The truth, Mairena once told his friends, is that the man was quite capable of all the exploits and the prodigies which he claimed for himself. That he had an in-

*Ramón del Valle-Inclán (1866–1936). Best known for his four novellas, or "sonatas," purporting to be the memoirs of the Marquis de Bradomín, Galician Don Juan; his cutting *esperpentos,* or farcical pieces; and his personal legend as artist, *galán,* and soldier of fortune.

nate gift of authority is unquestionable. If he was not, as he tells us, appointed Honorary Major of the Army of the Hot Countries, the fault is entirely Mexico's; for there was never better timber for an office of high command. Nevertheless, his real mark as a man is not his military heroism but his sanctity: his passion for ennobling life and his burning zeal for salvation. However much he may have preferred to save himself by the sword, it is his pen that will prove to be his salvation. Valle-Inclán will come to be known as the saint of our letters.

A saint of belles-lettres: such indeed was Valle-Inclán—a man who immolated his humanity and transformed it into literature of the highest order of excellence. We must read him and ponder him well, marveling at his incomparable pages. We shall discover that the author of these pages was not Valle-Inclán per se but an apocryphal creation of their author's. Of that good D. Ramón del Valle, beloved friend and unfailing teacher, I would say this chiefly: that he sought, above all other things, to be a knight without covet or servility. Let us forget, for the time being, the spate of anecdotes about his life and take note of the fastidious and, to my way of thinking, profoundly devout manner of his dying: his thundering ultimatum to his survivors that they take care to bury him outside the sanctions of the Church. How few could have foreseen it! There, in the beauties of Compostela, with its cathedral and its chapter house, its archbishop, and great incense burner—what a magnificent setting for the interment of a Bradomín! But for Valle-Inclán, the saintly inventor of Bradomín, the first obligation was to truth and not to fantasy. His last words ring with all the restlessness of the poet and the captain: "How long it all takes!" Don Ramón, how nobly you bore all things, to the end: to that last cup of which Manrique once sang!

XLII

¶ To tell the truth, Mairena said to his students, our perception of things past, which we call memory, is as inexplicable as our vision of things to come, which we call prophecy, divination, vaticination. It has never been established—far from it!—that our brain preserves vestigial impressions miraculously empowered to reproduce or actualize antecedent images. And even if we could grant the existence of these vestiges endowed with such a power, we should soon find that memory poses the same problem for us as perception—a problem, as I have explained on another occasion, which nobody has so far resolved. Just as we have learned to look upon memory without astonishment, we ought not to be too astounded by the vision of the future which some claim to possess. In each instance, we are confronted with the unexplained or, it may be, the inexplicable. At the very least, I would direct your amazement upon three things: memory, perception, and vaticination, without favor to any one of them. That way you will gain in enlightened ignorance—or rather, sympathetic ignorance—whatever you lose in fictitious or tentative learning.

¶ Question everything, like children. "Why this? And why this? And why that over there?" Here in Spain nobody ever converses, because nobody really asks questions except for the pleasure of answering them himself. We all want to hurry back from places we have never been to. We are all essentially yokels. Keep your questions coming, I beg of you—with no thought of the apparent absurdity of your queries. You will soon come to understand that the absurd is almost always a peculiarity of answerers. Because I can never forget that I am a professor of rhetoric, gentlemen, whose mission it is not to mold orators but, on the contrary, men of fair speech—provided they have something worth saying—you shall never learn from me how to embellish the vacuity of your thinking.

℄ Let us leave all talk of watches, those instruments of sophistry which seek to enmesh time with mathematics. As poets, delighting in poetry—nightingale's apprentices—what should we know of mathematics? Very little, indeed. And the little that we know quite suffices us. There is no need to count out our syllables, as in Berceo, or submit our verses to the yardstick; for the plectra of the young must be spared all vexation. And as metaphysicians—for that is our wish in the end—we have nothing to gain from mathematics; for nothing of *that which exists* can be counted or measured. Our watches have nothing to tell us about time—the psychical character of ultimate reality—which similarly rejects measure and number. Our watches only make us potter our reality away, till we come to think of all time as a trivial kind of impatience in which we wait for the tock that should always follow the tick. That is another of the illusions which we attribute to watches for which there is no foundation whatsoever.

XLIII

¶ Mairena was talking to his students: On the last day of all, as my teacher once said, art, science, and religion will all have to stand before the tribunal of logic. We must therefore reinforce our own logic, as a function of our sophistry, by submitting it to every conceivable test before the tribunal of itself. The position is not one original to us but to the ancient Greeks; for, as someone very pithily remarked, God created the Greeks so that generations of teachers to come would have bread and a livelihood.

¶ At the great roulette table of our facts it is hard to turn up with the right answers, and those who habitually play often leave it well plucked. At the very smallest wheel of our reasoning it is possible for a handful of questions to break the bank of our answers: that is why, my teacher went on to say, we attach such importance to questions. That is the coin that always comes to hand. Our problem is to ascertain whether our chips buy us anything of use in the end.

¶ All uncertainty is fruitful, as I have often pointed out to you, so long as it is accompanied by the wish to understand. On the road of the still uncomprehending, we comprehend something important—if only that we have come to *un*comprehend utterly something else we thought we had mastered. Pondering the fourth dimension of space, for example, I came to doubt the other three; I discovered that space as I previously thought of it —a great vacuum empty of matter, a primordial nothingness predating all bulk and imaginable geometrical form—might well have no dimensionality at all. On the day that I ascribe three dimensions to space, I reasoned, what is to keep me from granting it a fourth?

ℭ *On Bécquer*

The poetry of Bécquer,* Mairena was telling his students, so transparent and luminous, where everything seems set down for the express purpose of being understood, still has a charm quite apart from its logical tidiness. It uses the word in its time, that irreversible time of the psyche from which nothing more can be inferred or deduced. A principle of contradictions, properly speaking, seems to govern his discourse: yes; but then again, no; the swallows will come back, but then, they will not. How far removed we are, in the world of Bécquer, from that frightful machine of the syllogism laboring under the dense and intricated imagery of our country's illustrious baroque! Bécquer a Sevillian? Yes, but in the style of Velázquez, that cager and bewitcher of time. More of that later. Now let us hold in our minds Gustavo Adolfo—he of the meager rhymes, the ambiguous assonance, and the four verbs for every qualifying adjective. As someone wittily put it, Bécquer, that accordion played on by angels. I agree: by the angel of authentic poetry.

ℭ *On local time*

Reading all that is written today of the modern theory of relativity, Mairena would have exclaimed: "What an ingenious device for stopping the clock of divinity itself!" To speak truthfully: a God who was not, like my teacher's, ubiquity itself—what irreparable blunders in judging the order of events would he not loose upon the world!

---

*Gustavo Adolfo Bécquer (1836–1870). Best known for the lapidary lyricism of his *Rimas* and a collection of *Leyendas* in prose.

XLIV

❡ In everything that changes there is something which remains intact—that is to say, which does not change. This we generally call substance. But if the only changes possible are changes of place and motion, we would have to put it another way: in all motion there is something which remains immobile; substance is the immovable factor in all movement. The proposition is not only self-contradictory, but seems to contradict itself increasingly the more logically we attempt to express it: substance is that which, changing place, remains in its place and, moving, remains unmoved. Obviously our scientists would laugh such lucubrations to scorn, for they have already rejected the reality of substance and committed themselves to a postulate of motion. For them there is nothing objectionable about postulating movement without thinking of something movable. What they are really maintaining is this: if a subsistent—or a subexistent—entity should exist that we know nothing of, it would in effect *not* exist for us and there would be no basis for predicating either its motion or repose; still less in the case of an entity which does not in fact exist. Thus the whole realm of substance, and with it the movement of substance, is in effect put out to pasture. What is left us is motion as such, pure motion divorced from all substance: motion in which nothing moves or is moved, not even nothingness itself.

❡ Let us suspend for the time being all ratiocination, which is only the corrosive analysis of words after all. We live perforce in a world structured on a handful of words; and if we destroy those we have, we will have to substitute others. They are the true atlases of our world; if but one of them fails before its time, a whole universe is lost.

❡ Insecurity, uncertainty, and misgiving are perhaps the only truths left us. We must hold fast to them all. We can never know for a certainty whether the sun will rise for us tomorrow as it did for us today; or, if it does, whether it will appear at its accustomed station, since such points can hardly be ascertained with astronomical exactitude—assuming, indeed, that they actually exist. Even if you dismiss all such doubts as mere ratiocination—in the end, out-and-out pedantry—the doubt that we shall ever see tomorrow's sunrise must always be yielded. Insecurity is our mother; misgiving is our muse. If we turn into poets in the end, it is because, convinced of these things, we know we have good cause to sing and carry the burden with us. Or, if you prefer, because we are well aware of the evils that we seek to dispel with our song.

¶ Still, we must always ask, in advance of all other questions which might be posed for us, whether, if we confess our metaphysical misgivings, we are really capable of sincerely taking a stance. And having raised the question, let us answer with a simple shrug of the shoulders. If our question has any meaning at all, its scope would compel us to press on further and use it to the hilt. Chess master, must you really lose sleep mapping out every move that the knight may execute on the board before being checked by a castle? Is it a fact, you singers of the lilies of the field, that the smell of fried sausage means nothing to you? Where do such questions lead us? For underneath them all, whether of our own making or not, lies a perverse and surly abyss: the suspicion or, I dare say, the hope that human truth—whatever we held in sincerity—actually embodies all that is shabbiest, vilest, and most uncouth in mankind.

¶ For our own part, we are disposed to affirm the dignity of man and regard that as the noblest, the most intimate, and the most potent resource of his conduct. For this very mistrust of our own destiny, these mental misgivings, absent perhaps in all other animals, are joined in man to a life will that is more than a wish to preserve his own being—it is a determination to better it as well. Man is the only animal who yearns for salvation without surrendering himself forthwith to due process of nature. All his spiritual powers are mustered and marshaled to this end. For man would be *other*wise. That is the essence of the specifically human. Even while his native logic and sophistry close him into the narrowest solipsistic conception, the solitary monad within can never be considered self-sufficing, but moved by a nostalgia for the Other, sick with incurable mutability.

℄ Let me repeat what I have so often told you in the past: always take me with a grain of salt; I have no stock of truths to reveal to you. Nor would I have you assume that my purpose as a teacher is to induce you to mistrust your own thinking; I prefer, rather, to lay bare the mistrust which I have for my own. Disregard the air of conviction which I frequently employ with you, which is only a rhetorical or grammatical gambit of language, and my somewhat disrespectful and cavalier manner in alluding from time to time to great minds of the past. They are only the peevish affectations of a doddering orator in the most provincial sense of the word. Give them a deaf ear.

℄ Having said so much, let us move on to other matters. The tree of our culture, leafy or bare as the case may be, in whose topmost branches you may presently ensconce yourself, has no sap but our life's blood; only by chance do its roots reach out to the lecture halls of our schools, academies, universities, and so on. I mention this, not to warn you in advance against the lugubrious solemnity of the classroom that may some day burden your spirits, or to enjoin you never to enter them. I am far from thinking that either culture or wisdom is necessarily a blithe vocation like a child's game. It is quite possible that even children, for whom play is apparently a highly spontaneous activity, learn nothing by playing: not even, I dare say, how to play.

℄ Shoemaker, to your last, as they say! You may well ask: "And what is my last?" And, to avoid unfortunate confusion in the future, you may well ask me, in turn: "And what, pray, is yours?"

XLV

℄ *Mairena's greatcoat*

On the very bitterest days of winter Juan de Mairena wore a coarse greatcoat that he used to call his *Catalan vengeance,* because it was made of a Catalan fabric that weights the wearer without warming him. The peculiarity of this overcoat, Mairena used to tell his students is that, when brushed, it whisks out more dust than it ever whisks away, because a natural avidity for dust particles has rendered the nap overly absorbent and a dusty deposit was long ago packed into the weave of the fiber itself. The further fact that I was never much of a hand with the whisk broom may also have something to do with it. Let me say, however, I have since given some thought to the problem of conserving and tidying these coats—my own and others like it—even to the point of imagining a machine for the extraction of dust particles, a mixture of bristles and cantharides, directly applied to the fabric. My apparatus was a total failure for the same reason that all such devices for the correction of manifest botches generally fail: the less costly possibility of replacing my invention with an article of better quality. Not that my extracting apparatus failed to extract the dust from the fabric—far from it; but it took the cloth with it as well: literally pulverized it.

To get to my point, gentlemen: I should like to allegorize with this greatcoat, which I still suffer myself to wear, something of what we call culture which burdens so many without warming them. We zealously seek to defend it somehow against all those who, naked of culture themselves, would snatch it out of our grasp—or so we think. Bah! For my own part, if I have such a garment at all, I fear nothing from lurking coat snatchers, nor do I think there will be many to challenge my right to wear it till the end of my days.

℄ Though I consider myself a modest enough man, Mairena went on to say, I have no particular brief to make for the modesty of man. Let us be clear about this. I have never thought it necessary to regard man as either modest or moderate—and least of all, insignificant. Properly speaking, it is not man but his world which is insignificant. How easily we can at will, first, think a world; second, imagine it; third, measure it; fourth, doubt its existence; fifth, efface it; sixth, think about other things.

℄ Romanticism, my teacher used to say, has always been coupled with the notion of an age of gold which elegists like to refer to the past, and progressivists to a more or less nebulous future. They are two modes of romanticism: one aristocratic and the other popular, sometimes merging and mingling and at other times alternating, depending on the temper of the times. Underlying both is the classical mode of romanticism, which is our own, with its constantly querulous note of: But where will it all end?

℄ If we can imagine ourselves for the moment forced to select one poet from among all others, I would choose Shakespeare, that gigantic creator of consciousnesses. Shakespeare is perhaps the unique instance in which the genius of the modern seems to have outstripped the ancients. The translation of Shakespeare must be the most taxing of enterprises, given the great plenitude of his vocabulary, the freedom of his syntax, with its fondness for oblique or eliptical discourse in which so much more is inferred than is ever expressed. How difficult to render in a strange tongue the language which produced a work of art as vital and as incorrect as Shakespeare's! The French tend to translate his English by impoverishing it: they level it—literally iron it out as they go. One might almost say they try to translate him by explaining him away: "What poor Shakespeare meant to say was this . . ." For the Shakespearian mode has no real equivalence in the French poetical genius. Perhaps here in Spain we are better able to understand him. In any event, it is no easy matter to render poetically even in our own tongue his true depths as a poet—skeptical, nihilistic, agnostic—together with his enormous feeling for the human. To translate this paragon of Englishmen—is Shakespeare English, or is England Shakespearean?—we would have to know more English than the English and more Spanish than is common to us today. I say this with no wish to disparage recent translations, which are among the very finest. On the contrary, I would like to impress upon you how difficult it would be to excel them.

XLVI

¶ Let us talk about Chaos, gentlemen, which is our theme for today. My teacher, Mairena went on to tell his students, once composed a philosophical poem in the manner of the old Hellenic *Periphyseos,* which he called "Cosmos"; the first canto, entitled "Chaos," was the most understandable of all. There, he maintained, in effect, that God could never have created the world, if the world is indeed an aspect of His innate divinity; that the true act of creation, as he always insisted, was Nothingness. Nevertheless, for those who demand a mythological exposition of the divine, he conjured up a Genesis of his own: "God undertook to do nothing, really, since before the definitive Creation nothing needed to be done. What happened was this, simply: God beheld Chaos, saw that it was good, and said: "Let us call that the World." That is all.

¶ The truth is, said my teacher, that Chaos exists only in our own heads. We have planted it there in the sweat of our brows—doddering dominies that we are—to gratify our extravagant passion for tidying things up before translating them.

¶ *For a biography of Mairena*

Let me tell you the most important incident in my personal history. While still just a boy, I was out walking one day with my mother with a stick of sugar cane in my hand. It was in Seville, in the vanished days of a Christmas. Not far from me walked another mother with another child, also holding fast to a stalk of sugar cane. I was quite certain that mine was the largest—absolutely convinced of it! Nevertheless, I turned to my mother and I asked, as children will do, to confirm even their own first-hand evidence: "Mine's the biggest, isn't it?" "No, child," my mother answered me. "Have you no eyes in your head?" I have been asking myself that question all the rest of my life.

Another anecdote, also important, this time bearing on my prenatal life. Some dolphins, losing their way and coasting the tides, had penetrated to the Guadalquivir, coming as far inland as Seville. A crowd had gathered on the river bank from all parts of the city, attracted by the extraordinary spectacle—young girls and lovers, among them my parents, who had come to see it all for the first time. It was a sunny afternoon, which I have since fancied, or dreamed, I can remember at times.

℄ Very probably, our self-love separates us from the love of God. Certainly it keeps us from knowing the true depths of our being. On the outermost bounds of our self-hate, however, without pressing beyond them (for passion subverts understanding) other truths also await us—the most interesting truths of them all, it may be.

℄ The cult of the female nude is proper to poetry. In the female nude, poets often embody the very perfection of their art. That is all very fine. One should never forget, in the meantime, that the truly erotic sensibility, in evoking the image of woman, never omits to clothe it. The robing and disrobing: that is the true traffic of love.

℄ Remember Goya, the erotic master of Aragon. Why was it, do you think, that Goya painted his *maja* or courtesan in the nude? I give you Lope in answer: in order to

> [imagine her] clothed: that
> waist of such comely
> proportions; on her balcony
> poised high on her heels.

And vice versa? Why did he paint her fully clothed? So that we might all reimagine the pith of the feminine—ah!—under the clothing, *in puris naturabilis,* as the Latinists say.

℄ Though Gongorism is insipid, Góngora* himself was a poet: in all that he wrote breathes the gust of true poetry. You will have to measure him out in meters when the wind is right.

℄ *Mairena prophesies the European War*

After the blasphemies of Nietzsche, Mairena went on, nothing benign can be augured for the old Europe of which we are part —luckily a somewhat marginal part, a tail-end still to be flayed, as it were. Christ abandons us, saddened and shamed. Seminal, Biblical humanity bellows aloud, drunk on the pride of its procreative zoölogical fatuity. Do you hear the ullulations? Terrible wars are at hand.

℄ *Nietzsche and Schopenhauer*

Nietzsche had neither the genius nor the metaphysical inventiveness of Schopenhauer—neither the grace nor the good humor of the great pessimist. He is considerably less entertaining to read, even though Schopenhauer is always the systematic philosopher and Nietzsche virtually a poet. Nevertheless, we have his invention of an "Eternal Return" in the age of Carnot himself; his tone, at once resolute and poignant when confronting the improbable, has its own kind of greatness. The wild boar of a Zarathustra is a truly staggering creation. Nietzsche had both the talent and the cunning of the authentic psychologist—an uncommon virtue in his countrymen—of a man who saw deeply into himself and then pelted his fellowmen with his own entrails. He epitomizes for all time that psychology of resentment which ages and debases mankind. Read him as a master of aphorism and epigram.

For example:

> Beware the delicate hand:
> it destroys all
> that falls into it.

---

*Luis de Góngora (1561–1627). Better known for the cultivated intricacies of his later *Soledades* than for his romances in popular balladic style.

❨ My teacher loved the old cities of Spain, in whose deserted streets he was fond of prowling at small hours of the morning, disturbing the peace of the alley cats, who fled in fear at his passing. Yet he was a naturally gregarious man who rarely turned the key in his lock without stopping to chat with the old neighborhood night watchman.

"No one comes this way, I suppose?"

"Only you and the alley cats."

"That old cloak of yours, now: is it warm enough?"

"Warm enough, sir."

"But when the temperature drops?"

"Then I slip into this doorway and huddle up—so—in my clothing, with the lantern between my legs."

"So, the lamp keeps you warm?"

"What else!"

"You're a true philosopher."

"We learn by living, sir."

"Good night."

"Good night."

XLVII

ℭ Whenever I hear of the death of a poet, I tell myself: How often in the service of his craft must he not have invoked death, without ever quite believing it! And what would he think now seeing it emerge from his own jack-in-the-box as the last surprise of them all!

ℭ It ill becomes us to deal rhetorically with a subject as somber as death. Nevertheless, it has often been said that the greatness of Socrates was never more apparent than when, biding his time for the hemlock, he launched an immortal dialogue on the theme of death in which there is no trace whatsoever of solemnity. "One more dialogue, even though it be my last. But first, will someone kindly escort that woman home!"

ℭ After all, my teacher said, Socrates was perhaps a bit cruel and unjust to Xantippe, who for once in her life may have wanted to rise to the occasion in her own way!

ℭ Are we so certain of death that we have ceased to give it any thought at all? We do think about death. Death is the preoccupation par excellence of everybody, the theme most constant in our thought. We carry it in our thinking in that innocuous zone of the spirit wherein nothing can frighten us or induce us to hope any longer. The truth is, we have come to give it our thought, and then ceased to believe in it as a fact.

ℭ When we read in the papers of great battles in which thousands upon thousands perish, how can we close our eyes to the carnage and sleep through a night? Yet sleep we do, and wake up the following morning with a head full of other matters. Are we, then, utterly lacking in imagination? For if but a dog—much less a man!—die at our side, we are ready to shed bitter tears; our sympathy and our charity go with it. For us, as for Galileo, nature writes a mathematical language that is the language of contemplation; and tragedy, arithmetically computed, leaves us unmoved. Do we need, then, hired mourners for our wars, coming all disheveled, like mothers, their babes in their arms, and shrieking: "Enough of wars!" Yet that, too, would come to little. There will always be an imperious voice—which is not Socrates'!—commanding all women to silence: "Silence! The cannon are about to speak!"

¶ Be men of bad taste. I urge you to be men of bad taste if we are ever to check the excesses of passing fashion. Bad taste is often identified with what is currently unfashionable; yet, dare to be unfashionable, and you may yet find what suits your style best.

XLVIII

❡ Life—outside the laboratory—is never an idea, but a datum of immediate consciousness, a turbulent manifestation of being. How else explain the optimism of the Irishman in the anecdote who, hurled into space from a height of five stories, kept on saying in his ever accelerating plunge to the cobbles below by the directest possible route: "So far, all's well!"

❡ I will never exhort you to "write it all down"; the main thing is to speak and make known to your neighbor what you feel and you think. Writing, on the contrary, is an infraction of the natural norm, a sin against the nature of our spirits. But if you turn into writers in the end, be simple stenographers of the spoken thought. Never hoard what you write down. The unpublished manuscript is like an unconfessed sin that festers in the soul, corrupting and contaminating it. God keep you from the malice of the unpublished!

❡ The ineffable charm of all poetry, which, as many have pointed out, is an outcome of words, is freely given as a dividend of direct and felicitous utterance. "Naturalness"? I have no wish to expose you to the vested ill will of the virtuosi by bringing up that discredited word. Nature, after all, is only one alphabet in the language of poetry. Is there a better one? The "natural" in poetry is usually the well-spoken and in general the most elegant solution of the problem of expression. "Quod elixum est ne assato," a Pythagorean proverb tells us; and some day another voice may say with more ambitious exactitude:

> Not a stroke more!
> There's the whole of your rose!

Bear in mind that in poetry—above all, in poetry—all our twisting and turning is a mode of our avid search for the shortest possible way, for direct utterance; that tropes, which confound and becloud instead of clarifying and embellishing, are superfluous; and that our most enduring allusions to the human condition are always made in the language of Everyman.

XLIX

¶ Señor de Mairena made a practice of always setting his watch back twenty-four hours. It was his way of solving the difficult problem of living in the past and meeting his current engagements punctually when necessary. Still, it must have been a little disconcerting to hear twelve strike in the still of the night, consult one's watch, and exclaim: "What a bother! Twelve, already!" But later to add, with a smile: "But twelve o'clock yesterday, by my watch!" (From an article entitled *Bagatelles* and signed Quasimodo, in *El Mercantil Gaditano,* May 12, 1895.)

¶ Of our surrealists, Juan de Mairena might well have remarked: "All these jackasses turning wheels at the draw well: do they understand that where there are wells there should be water?"

¶ Those who have nothing to say to any man have nothing to say to mankind; and those who say nothing to mankind have no one to talk to at all.

¶ In the last analysis, there will always be a somebody face to face with a something: a something that seems to have no need of anyone—no one at all.

¶ Between Nietzsche and his successors stands the European World War, a war whose victors will never be known to us perhaps—if we have not, indeed, all ended as losers.

¶ In the aftermath of that war Juan de Mairena predicted that there would follow a total collapse of the "masses." There are too many already jamming the garrisons, those great monasteries of the modern, he maintained, too many busily turning out howitzers and war machines in our factories: men whose sole mission it seems to be to rid all Europe of its excess population. After a clash of such magnitude, no one will dare to speak of the masses for fear of the machine guns. What Mairena failed to understand was that the masses are, among other lamentable things, a revelation of the machine guns.

L

℄ If we doubt the whole world of appearance and regard it as the veil of Maya hiding from our sight the realm of absolute reality, it can hardly matter greatly if the veil were one day to rend, showing us absolute reality. Could we be sure that discovered reality was not actually another veil, destined in its turn to rend and reveal to us another and another? Or putting it a little differently, an illusion of the illusory character of our world might always accompany our passage into the realest of all possible worlds. However, no one can prevent us from taking the contrary position—to wit, that the veils of appearance, though multiplied to infinity, actually veil nothing; that nothing waits to reveal itself behind the apparent; and that the only abiding reality in the end is appearance itself. Putting it still another way: our belief in the reality of the world could always accompany our passage into the most illusory of all possible worlds. The world as illusion and the world as reality are equally undemonstrable. What is unfortunate is not our awareness of an antinomy in which thesis and antithesis seem equally plausible, and that this inanity might lead us to yield to a principle of contradiction in the end. In that event, it is our mistrust, rather than the tribunal of logic, that speaks. The disquieting thing lies not in our inability to pursue one or the other alternative, by some prodigious exercise of reason, but in our restless ambivalence between two contradictory beliefs.

℄ Those of us who insist on the impossibility of a creation *ex nihilo*, for theological and metaphysical reasons, are not therefore obliged to renounce a creative God capable of realizing such a prodigy. For the great feat of having wrested a world out of nothing is no greater than that which my teacher attributed to his own deity—the feat of having wrested Nothing out of the world. Reflect on that theme: for our studies are now at an end, and it is time that we broadened our questions, like the broadening of a sail, if we are ever to make for the open seas of contemplation.

APPENDIX

Los Cancioneros Apócrifos

ABEL MARTÍN

Dijo Dios: Brote la nada.
Y alzó la mano derecha,
hasta ocultar su mirada.
Y quedó la nada hecha.

I: *Siesta*

(*En memoria de Abel Martín*)

Mientras traza su curva el pez de fuego,
junto al ciprés, bajo el supremo añil,
y vuela en blanca piedra el niño ciego,
y en el olmo la copla de marfil
de la verde cigarra late y suena,
honremos al Señor
—la negra estampa de su mano buena—
que ha dictado el silencio en el clamor.

Al Dios de la distancia y de la ausencia,
del áncora en el mar, la plena mar . . .
Él nos libra del mundo —omnipresencia—
nos abre senda para caminar.

Con la copa de sombra bien colmada,
con este nunca lleno corazón,
honremos al Señor que hizo la Nada
y ha esculpido en la fe nuestra razón.

From The Apocryphal Songbooks:

ABEL MARTÍN

And God said: "Let NOTHING bring forth!"
and He raised His right hand
to blot out the sight from His vision. And
NOTHING conceived upon earth.

I: *Siesta*

In memory of Abel Martín

While fish blazon their burning parabolas
in sovereign indigo, there by the cypress-stand,
and a blind boy flies, a white stone climbing the air,
and the green cicada scratches his sounding pulsation
in the ivory turns of a ballad, high in the elms:
praise we the Lord–
the black intaglio of His provident hand
that orders the word and the silence after the word.

Master of distance and absence alike, O
anchor plumbing the water, and water's abundance . . .
He shall deliver us all from the world, He will open
the way to the walker in the might of His omnipresence.

Surely our cup runneth over, our cup runneth over with shade.
Now, with insatiable hearts, affirming our drouth,
praise we the Lord, Who fashioned the Null and the Void
and chiseled the block of our reason into our faith.

II: *Dos Canciones*

(A la manera de Abel Martín)

1

Abre el rosal de la carroña horrible
su olvido en flor, y extraña mariposa,
jade y carmín, de vuelo imprevisible,
salir se ve del fondo de una fosa.
Con el terror de víbora encelada,
junto al lagarto frío,
con el absorto sapo en la azulada
libébula que vuela sobre el río,
con los montes de plomo y de ceniza,
sobre los rubios agros
que el sol de mayo hechiza,
se ha abierto un abanico de milagros
—el ángel del poema lo ha querido—
en la mano creadora del olvido . . .

II: *Two Songs*

In the manner of Abel Martín

1

The rose-tree, out of carrion horror, bares
oblivion's blossoms, and the dubious moth,
crimson and crocus, in unforeseeable air,
stirs in the middens and shows himself from the depths.
So, with a covetous serpent's terror
and the cold keep of the lizard,
the toad's avidity follows the dragonfly's color,
bluing the air of the river;
mountains are ashen or leaden,
charmed in the wan domain
that mid-May's sunlight maddens,
while, for angel's sake and singer's,
oblivion's living fingers
widen the miraculous fan.

2

Que apenas si de amor el ascua humea
sabe el poeta que la voz engola
y, barato cantor, se pavonea
con su pesar o enluta su viola;
y que si amor da su destello, sola
la pura estrofa suena,
fuente de monte, anónima y serena.
Bajo el azul olvido, nada canta,
ni tu nombre ni el mío, el agua santa.
Sombra no tiene de su turbia escoria
limpio metal; el verso del poeta
lleva ansia de amor que lo engendrara
como lleva el diamante sin memoria
—frío diamante— el fuego del planeta
trocado en luz, en una joya clara . . .

2

Grazed by love's smoking coal,
the poet will prate of his talent,
tuning the whine of his viol,
his doldrums and caterwaul,
to the maudlin catch of a ballad.
Should love strike a light in us,
none but the pure line sounds,
headsprings out of the ground,
stilled and anonymous.
In that oblivious blue
the blessed waters sing
nothing of me or you
or any living thing.
Immaculate metals shun
the dross and dark of the slag:
the poem is well-begun
that sings, as the passion begs,
love's ardor and despond,
shaping a planet's fire,
light's always altering fuel,
to the freezing cut of a stone,
the limpid play in the jewel,
the unmemoried diamond.

III: Últimas Lamentaciones de Abel Martín

Hoy, con la primavera,
soñé que un fino cuerpo me seguía
cual dócil sombra. Era
mi cuerpo juvenil, el que subía
de tres en tres peldaños la escalera.
—*Hola, galgo de ayer.* (Su luz de acuario
trocaba el hondo espejo
por agria luz sobre un rincón de osario.)
—*¿Tú, conmigo, rapaz?*
—*Contigo, viejo.*

Soñé la galería
al huerto de ciprés y limonero;
tibias palōmas en la piedra fría,
en el cielo de añil rojo pandero,
y en la mágica angustia de la infancia
la vigilia del ángel más austero.

La ausencia y la distancia
volví a soñar con túnicas de aurora;
firme en el arco tenso la saeta
del mañana, la vista aterradora
de la llama prendida en la espoleta
de su granada . . .

III: *Abel Martín: Last Lamentations*

This spring day, I dreamed
that a delicate body, my amenable
double in shadow, moved with me. The body
of boyhood it seemed,
leaping the treads of a stairway, three at a bound.
  —*You, there! You, yesterday's greyhound!*
(A light like a lighted aquarium,
sea-change of mirrors, that deepened
its rancid effulgence in a carrion corner of ashes.)
  —*Still with me, young playfellow?*
                                        —*Still with you, old father!*

And dreamed then the gallery
and the garden of cypress and lemons:
a languishing pigeon warming the cold of a stone,
red kites on the indigo-blues;
and that ward of my childhood, austerest angel of all,
keeping watch on a magical anguish.

Absence and distance,
the tunics of morning: I could tell
them again in my dream—poised taut on a bow-line's resistance,
day's arrow, the vision that ends in a scream:
the burst of the flame in the fuse
and the charge in the shell . . .

IV: *Muerte de Abel Martín*

1

Los últimos vencejos revolean
en torno al campanario;
los niños gritan, saltan, se pelean.
En su rincón, Martín el solitario.
¡La tarde, casi noche, polvorienta,
la algazara infantil, y el vocerío,
a la par de sus doce en sus cincuenta!

¡Oh alma plena y espíritu vacío,
ante la turbia hoguera
con llama restallante de raíces,
fogata de frontera
que ilumina las hondas cicatrices!

Quien se vive se pierde, Abel decía.
¡Oh distancia, distancia!, que la estrella
que nadie toca, guía.
¿Quién navegó sin ella?

Distancia para el ojo—¡oh lueñe nave!—
ausencia al corazón empedernido,
y bálsamo suave
con la miel del amor, sagrado olvido.
¡Oh gran saber del cero, del maduro
fruto sabor que sólo el hombre gusta,
agua de sueño, manantial oscuro,
sombra divina de la mano augusta!
Antes me llegue, si me llega, el Día,
la luz que ve, increada,
ahógame esta mala gritería,
Señor, con las esencias de tu Nada.

IV: *Death of Abel Martín*

1

Circling the bell-tower,
the martlets, trailing, soar;
children are storming the air and crying, at their wars.
Adept in his solitude, Martín, in a corner there.
Evening or twilight making, dust,
and a squabble of voices, a child's vociferations,
fifty or twelve, however you make it, all's one.

O starveling-spirit and prodigal of soul,
by the glowering bonfire's circle
where dead sticks crackle in a fiery air
and blazon a blind frontier,
showing its blackest cicatrices clear!

The living shall surely perish, as Abel said.
Ah, distance, distance! the star
that none may handle, yet lightens the way ahead:
shall any voyage prosper, lacking it?

Great eye that looks on distance—O lessening sail!
heart indurate in absence,
bland herbs
and honeys of love, blessed in forgetfulness.
Lore of the mastering Zero, of the rounded
fruit's quintessence, ripening for man's need,
gout that breaks in a dream, and fountainhead of shadow,
shadow of godhead under the stretched, dread hand!
Before it be Day, if day be given, indeed,
the all-beholding light, that is not yet come to pass,
whelm what is vile in me, out-cry and exhortation,
Lord of all essences, and drown me in Nothingness.

2

El ángel que sabía
su secreto salió a Martín al paso.
Martín le dió el dinero que tenía.
¿Piedad? Tal vez. ¿Miedo al chantaje? Acaso.
Aquella noche fría
supo Martín de soledad; pensaba
que Dios no le veía,
y en su mudo desierto caminaba.

3

Y vió la musa esquiva,
de pie junto a su lecho, la enlutada,
la dama de sus calles, fugitiva,
la imposible al amor y siempre amada.
Díjole Abel: Señora,
por ansia de tu cara descubierta,
he pensado vivir hacia la aurora
hasta sentir mi sangre casi yerta.
Hoy sé que no eres tú quien yo creía;
mas te quiero mirar y agradecerte
lo mucho que me hiciste compañía
con tu frío desdén.
Quiso la muerte
sonreír a Martín, y no sabía.

4

Viví, dormí, soñé y hasta he creado
—pensó Martín, ya turbia la pupila—
un hombre que vigila
el sueño, algo mejor que lo soñado.
Mas si un igual destino
aguarda al soñador y al vigilante,
a quien trazó caminos,
y a quien siguió caminos, jadeante,
al fin, sólo es creación tu pura nada,
tu sombra de gigante,
el divino cegar de tu mirada.

2

And that angel, skilled
in his secret, went out to Martín in the pass.
He gave him the little he had—the pietist's
pittance, perhaps?—or a sop for extortionists?
Perhaps. But Martín, there in the cold,
knew himself lonely, strove with his knowledge, reproved
the Omnipotent Knower Who had no eye for His child,
and all that night in unspeakable wilderness moved.

3

And saw his equivocal Muse
erect by his bedstead, the fugitive
haunting his streets, the bereft
and impossible love and the lady forever beloved.
And called to her: Lady,
for the uncovering of that face, my passion
thought to live until morning
though my heart's blood turn to suet.
Wisdom is given me now: you are other than I dreamt;
yet would I bless you still,
and gaze the more, however you walked at your will
at my side, in cold contempt.
Death turned to smile
at Martín, but knew no way to do it.

4

I lived, I drowsed, I dreamed—
Martín thought, while his pupils thickened—
and thereby conceived a man in a slumbering vigil
intent on his dream, beyond what is dreamt or imagined.
Yet, if a harder reckoning be wanting,
equal for dreamer and watcher alike, and the same
for those who apportion the roads
and those who follow them, panting,
conception in perfect nullity is yours, in the end:
the shadow of your presence, a colossus,
divinity left gazing at us blinded.

5

Y sucedió a la angustia la fatiga,
que siente su esperar desesperado,
la sed que el agua clara no mitiga,
la amargura del tiempo envenenado.
¡Esta lira de muerte!
Abel palpaba
su cuerpo enflaquecido.
¿El que todo lo ve no le miraba?
¡Y esta pereza, sangre del olvido!
¡Oh, sálvame, Señor!
Su vida entera,
su historia irremediable aparecía
escrita en blanda cera.
¿Y ha de borrarte el sol del nuevo dia?
Abel tendió su mano
hacia la luz bermeja
de una caliente aurora de verano,
ya en el balcón de su morada vieja.
Ciego, pidió la luz que no veía.
Luego llevó, sereno,
el limpio vaso, hasta su boca fría,
de pura sombra—¡oh, pura sombra!—lleno.

5

First anguish; then exhaustion,
the pangs of despairing assurance:
the unappeasable thirst no water may ever diminish,
wormwood of time made poisonous with durance.
That lyre stretched for his dying!
Abel made trial with his hand
of his emaciate body.
Beholder of all that exists, did His vision not see him there, lying?
O the sloth of it, bleeding oblivion!
Help me, Lord help me!
His life, from its beginnings,
the unchangeable fable of his being, hovered,
traced on the yielding wax.
Would he melt, with the coming of day, in the sun?
Abel lifted a hand
to the light
of the vehement morning, reddening into summer,
that burned on the balcony of his dimming habitation.
Blinded, he groped for the glimmer he had never discovered.
Then raised to his lips,
grown icier now, unhurried, the immaculate glass
of purest dark—O purest darkness!—brimming.

V: *Al Gran Pleno o Conciencia Integral*
(De "Los Complementarios" de Abel Martín)

Que en su estatua al alto Cero
—mármol frío,
ceño austero
y una mano en la mejilla—,
del gran remanso del río,
medite, eterno, en la orilla,
y haya gloria eternamente.
Y la lógica divina
que imagina,
pero nunca imagen miente
—no hay espejo; todo es fuente—,
diga: sea
cuanto es, y que se vea
cuanto ve. Quieto y activo
—mar y pez y anzuelo vivo,
todo el mar en cada gota,
todo el pez en cada huevo,
todo nuevo—,
lance unánime su nota.
Todo cambia y todo queda,
piensa todo,
y es a modo,
cuando corre, de moneda,
un sueño de mano en mano.
Tiene amor rosa y ortiga,
y la amapola y la espiga
le brotan del mismo grano.
Armonía;
todo canta en pleno día.
Borra las formas del cero,
torna a ver,
brotando de su venero,
las vivas aguas del ser.

V: *Greatness Abounding or Integral Consciousness*

From "The Complementaries" of Abel Martín

Let him ponder that sovereign Zero—statued
in bleakest marble
and frowning austerely,
one hand supporting its cheek—
by the wide backwaters of the river,
time without end, by the water's margin;
peace to his rest who slumbers forever and ever.
And that divinest logic
which imagines,
the undissembling image—
(enough of mirrors! the fountain-burst is all!)—
say it: let be whatever exists, let whatever
discloses itself be seen. Serene and strenuous
—the sea and the fish and the living hook for the fish,
the whole of the sea in a droplet, all
fish in the single egg,
and all of it new—let each
make its separate sign and be unanimous.
All keeps its appointed place, all moves
and reflects
and is changed like a changing coin as it goes:
a dream moving this way and that. Love
keeps the nettle, the rose;
the kernel of wheat and the poppy
bring it forth in a single seed.
That harmony! All sings
in the day's meridian:
effaces the faces of zero,
turns to its vision, seeing
where the bubble boils in the spring,
the vehement waters of being.